TROJAN EDDIE

a screenplay

Billy Roche was born and lives in Wexford, Ireland. He
began his career as a singer and musician, forming the
Roach Band in the late 70s before turning to acting and
writing. He is the author of numerous plays including *The
Wexford Trilogy*: *A Handful of Stars*, (Bush Theatre, 1988
– John Whiting Award, Plays and Players Award Best
Play, Thames Television Award), *Poor Beast in the Rain*
(Bush Theatre, 1989 – George Devine Award), *Belfry*
(Bush Theatre, 1991 – Charrington Fringe Award Best
Play, Time Out Theatre Award). *The Wexford Trilogy* also
performed at the Theatre Royal, Wexford and the Abbey
Theatre, Dublin and televised. Also the author of
Amphibians (RSC, 1992), *The Cavalcaders* (Abbey
Theatre). He has worked as an actor in *The Cavalcaders*
(Abbey Theatre), *A Handful of Stars* (Bush Theatre),
Aristocrats (Hampstead Theatre), *Poor Beast in the Rain*
(Abbey Theatre) and on television in *The Bill*. His films
include *Strapless* by David Hare.

TROJAN EDDIE

a screenplay by
Billy Roche

Methuen Film
in association with
Channel Four Television Corporation

A METHUEN SCREENPLAY

First published in Great Britain in 1997
by Methuen
Random House, 20 Vauxhall Bridge Road, London SW1V 2SA

Random House Australia (Pty) Limited
20 Alfred Street, Milsons Point, Sydney
New South Wales 2061, Australia

Random House New Zealand Limited
18 Poland Road, Glenfield, Auckland 10, New Zealand

Random House South Africa (Pty) Limited
Endulini, 5a Jubilee Road, Parktown 2193, South Africa

Random House UK Limited Reg. No. 954009

Distributed in the United States of America
by Heinemann, a division of Reed Elsevier Inc
361 Hanover Street, Portsmouth, New Hampshire NH 03901 3959

Copyright © 1997 by Billy Roche
Photographs copyright © 1997 by Jonathan Hession and Ari Ashley
All rights reserved

A CIP catalogue record for this book
is available at the British Library
ISBN 0 413 71800 X

Typeset in 10 on 13.5 point Plantin Light
by Wilmaset Ltd, Birkenhead, Wirral
Printed and bound in Great Britain
by Cox & Wyman Ltd, Reading, Berkshire

INTRODUCTION

When I first began working on *Trojan Eddie* I told myself, and everyone else who'd listen to me, that I wanted to write a script and subsequently make a picture that was as Irish as a French film is French and without too many nods to the language of Hollywood either – or anywhere else for that matter. I believed then, as I still do now, that if we are to create a genuine Irish film industry then we must use our own voice and trust that other people will be interested in what we have to say.

And so, inspired by the ancient Irish myth of Diarmuid and Grania, I set to work on *Trojan Eddie*, the story of an unlucky little fellow who rambles into the strange world of the Irish Traveller and finds himself trapped inside a tangled tale that is unfolding all around him.

And what a wonderful world it turned out to be as my research unearthed one glittering nugget after another. At times I felt like I was treading on foreign soil in my own homeland and simple wisdom was everywhere. 'That's why you'll never see a traveller with cataracts,' the legendary Pecker Dunne said to me one day as we stood around a smoky campfire, wiping the streaming tears from our eyes.

Travellers have their own unique culture – their own songs and stories, their own mode of dress, their own language even; which I know as Shelta – one of the secret languages of Ireland. I decided to make them the insiders of my story (they are usually portrayed as 'victims' or as 'outsiders' or worse again as the 'shunned'.) In this tale, it is Trojan Eddie, the settled one, who is on the outside.

John Power (played by Richard Harris) is the Fionn MacCumhal of the piece. He is a rich, powerful, settled Traveller who becomes besotted with Kathleen, a beautiful young Traveller. In some ways she reminds him of his late wife. In other ways she represents his youth and vitality. But more than all that she seems to be a link back to the old life that he has forsaken. For, in spite of his riches there is an underlining sadness about him – like a man who has lost his place in the tribe.

John Power offers to marry Kathleen and although she has a 'grá' for his young handsome nephew Dermot, she accepts, if only to escape the squalor of the trailer and the muck and the mire of the halting site. But on the wedding night she elopes with Dermot, taking with them the dowry money and Trojan Eddie, who works for John Power, gets caught up in a dangerous tale that he may not live to tell.

In the old myth Fionn MacCumhal actually wins back his Grania and Diarmuid is killed by a wild boar that is chased his way. And when the victorious Fionn rides into town with his young bride everybody laughs at his lovesick-foolishness. All these elements I tried to incorporate into a modern myth and this is what I passed on to Gillies Mackinnon, who then went deftly diving into the mythic waters to grapple with the funerals and the weddings and the fist fights and the faces that people this strange little love story.

> 'You think that you're in heaven
> But you haven't got a clue
> Love can take you to the stars
> Then love makes a fool of you.'

Billy Roche
Feb 1997

TROJAN EDDIE

CAST

TROJAN EDDIE	Stephen Rea
JOHN POWER	Richard Harris
DERMOT	Stuart Townsend
KATHLEEN	Aislin McGuckin
GINGER	Brendan Gleeson
RAYMIE	Sean McGinley
SHIRLEY	Angeline Ball
CAROL	Angela O'Driscoll
BETTY	Brid Brennan
PATSY MCDONAGH	Jason Gilroy
ROSY	Maria McDermottroe
GERRY	Sean Lawlor
LADY CASH	Britta Smith
MATT	Pat Laffan
REG	Jimmy Keogh
EDDIE'S MOTHER	Gladys Sheehan
ARTHUR	Noel Donovan
LANDLADY	Aoife MacEoin
TRAVELLER	Pecker Dunne
TRAVELLING WOMAN	Linda Quinn
RED-HAIRED TRAVELLER	Dolores Keane
YOUNG WOMAN	Orla Charlton
MAN	Billy Roche
PRIEST	Des Cave
SECOND TRAVELLER	Michael Collins
JENNY	Aisling O'Flanagan
REBECCA	Roisin O'Flanagan
LADY CASH'S SON	Eugene O'Brien
FARMER'S WIFE	Charlotte Bradley
Producer	Emma Burge
Director	Gillies Mackinnon
Screenplay	Billy Roche
Director of Photography	John de Borman
Production Designer	Frank Conway
Costume Designer	Consolata Boyle
Editor	Scott Thomas
Music	John Keane
Casting	John and Ros Hubbard

An Initial Films production in association with Irish Screen for Channel Four Films

INT. WAREHOUSE. DAY.

A warehouse-cum-auction room. Two men are up on a makeshift stage, surrounded by their wares – cassette players, duvets, portable phones, video games, cheap perfumes etc. A crowd is gathered beneath them. EDDIE, *the older man, is doing the selling while* DERMOT, *the younger man, does the running around – taking the goods to the customers and collecting the money and so on. The credits are rolling over the next few scenes.*

EDDIE: Do yeh see this razor. I tell yeh words cannot express my love for this razor. This is the Rolls-Royce of razors. Did yeh know that? It glides across your face like a hovercraft. It's cordless – light as a feather too. And talk about a close shave. I tell yeh, if it was any closer I'd have to sell it as a vibrator . . . (*To a woman in the front row.*) What are you laughin' at? I tell yeh, the first time I used this razor I liked it so much that I went out and knocked off the warehouse. No, seriously though. Seventy quid up the town. Needless to say I'm not askin' seventy. I'm not askin' sixty. Or fifty even. I'm not askin' forty. I'm not even askin' thirty for this beautiful machine. I'll tell yeh what I'm goin' to do. I'm goin' to let it go for ten. Who'll give me ten pounds for it? (*Hands in the air . . .*)

Ah, to hell with ten, I'm feelin' generous and that's a dangerous trait in my profession I don't mind tellin' yeh. There was an old trader called Patsy Murphy who died of it last year, yeh know. In fact that's what they put on his tombstone . . .

3

INT. DILAPIDATED BUILDING. STAIRWAY. DAY.

JOHN POWER *and his son* GINGER *enter a dreary hallway and begin to climb the stairs. The* LANDLADY *comes out to watch them from below.*

EDDIE (*v.o.*): '. . . Here Lies Patsy Murphy Who Died of Generosity on the twenty-fourth of May'. But, I'm a man who likes living dangerously, so I'll tell yeh what I'm gonna do. (JOHN *and* GINGER *hurry up the stairs.*) I'm gonna let this thing go for a fiver and I'm gonna throw in this little hand mirror so yeh can watch your lily-white skin while you're at it. Did I say a fiver?

DERMOT (*v.o.*): You did.

EDDIE (*v.o.*): No, I meant three.

INT. WAREHOUSE. DAY.

EDDIE (*shouts*): Yes, three pounds. Who'll give me three pounds? Yes, sold all right to the scruffy lookin' man down at the back. And boy do you need it! Here, Dermot . . . don't forget his mirror. (EDDIE *holds up mirror.*) Who's the fairest in the land? I don't think so . . .

INT. DILAPIDATED BUILDING. HALLWAY. DAY.

JOHN POWER *and* GINGER *are rapping on a bedroom door. The door opens and* RAYMIE *peeps out. His face drops.*

JOHN: How's it goin', Raymie?

RAYMIE: How's it goin'?

JOHN *pushes door open, walks past* RAYMIE *into room.* GINGER *follows.*

4

INT. WAREHOUSE. DAY.

EDDIE: Who'll give me two pounds for . . . Please sir, don't
put your hand up until yeh know what I have on my
mind. For you might not want what I'm sellin' and if I
point to you, and you have your hand in the air, then I'll
want my money regardless. Right?

INT. DILAPIDATED BUILDING. ROOM. DAY.
JOHN POWER, GINGER *and* RAYMIE *face each other.*
RAYMIE's *hand is in plaster.*

RAYMIE (*explaining his hand*): I dropped a fella up in The
Mermaid the other night. He went down like a ton of
bricks, broke a bone in me hand. The story of my life,
boy! Even when I win, I lose. Listen, er . . . um . . . I
haven't managed to shift that other thing yet, like, yeh
know. And I don't want to do anythin' hasty or
anythin'. I mean another couple of days should do it.
JOHN: Sure, it's been a week already, Raymie. I mean yeh
don't write, yeh don't phone. I mean – what am I
supposed to think, like?

INT. WAREHOUSE. DAY.

EDDIE: Who'll give me two quid for whatever's on my
mind? Anybody? Yes? You're prepared to give me two
pounds for whatever's on my mind? Well supposin' I
was to tell yeh that I had nothin' on my mind? Sure, it's
only two quid. Fair enough. Dermot, go get my money.
I wish everybody was like you. I'd be a millionaire by
now.
　　As it happens, I do have somethin' on my mind.
(*Shouts.*) As it happens, this is your lucky day. 'Cause

5

I'm goin' to give yeh this alarm clock. (EDDIE *throws an alarm clock to* DERMOT *who places it in dustbin liner*.) And I'm goin' to throw in this set of bone china for the parlour. Perfume from Paris for behind your ear. And some aftershave for the man in your life. A portable phone so you can give him a bell whenever yeh feel like checkin' up on him. A tool-box for the handyman. I thought you said you were handy. I'm handy, I only live around the corner.

INT. DILAPIDATED BUILDING. ROOM. DAY.

JOHN (*to* RAYMIE): I'll tell yeh what I'm goin' to do. I'll give yeh 'til tomorrow to get the money for me.

RAYMIE: Tomorrow?

JOHN: Aye, tomorrow. Wednesday, right?

RAYMIE: Huh?

GINGER (*to* JOHN): Tomorrow's Thursday.

JOHN: Thursday? Are yeh sure? (*Whispers*.) I thought tomorrow was Wednesday.

GINGER: Thursday.

JOHN: Well . . . in that case, Raymie, I'm afraid you're out of luck.

RAYMIE: Huh?

JOHN *gives* GINGER *the bend and with that* GINGER *head-butts* RAYMIE *who sinks to his knees with a cry of pain.*

INT. WAREHOUSE. DAY.

EDDIE: A tracksuit. A box full of the latest videos. An umbrella. And what about this beautiful ornament for the mantelpiece. Polar bear with young. Sheets and pillowcases.

7

DERMOT (*over*): What are yeh doin'?

EDDIE: Dermot, I'm gonna need another bag there.

DERMOT: What are yeh doin'? You're ruinin' us. Stop. That's enough.

EDDIE: Just get me another bag, will yeh? A Walkman! A duvet cover.

OLD WOMAN (*over*): Oh, Jesus!

EDDIE: Two electric blankets. An over and an under. And what about this beautiful lampshade, eh? Take it easy with that shade, Dermot, it's fragile.

DERMOT (*to* EDDIE): Like your brain.

EXT. WAREHOUSE. CAR PARK. DAY.

DERMOT *is helping the* YOUNG WOMAN *to her car with the black bags. He loads them into the boot, closes it, and steps towards her. She is enchanted by his primitive beauty.*

YOUNG WOMAN: Thanks.

DERMOT: Can I see yeh again some time?

YOUNG WOMAN: I don't know about that, I'm married.

DERMOT: Give us your number anyway. Sure who knows.

She thinks about it, sighs and then finally relents, reaching into her bag for a pen and paper. DERMOT *smiles.*

INT. WAREHOUSE. DAY.

EDDIE: You see the miracles that I perform here. Now I'm finished piddlin' around. I'm here to make money. And any man, woman, or child who's not prepared to spend at least fifty quid in this shop today should leave here and now.

Go on. Beat it! Go back from whence yeh came and quit wastin' my time here. 'Cause I'm goin' to lock the doors now and we're goin' to do some real business.

I'm looking for fifty pounds a head from each and every one of yeh. And then, I'm goin' to take the lot of you on a short trip up the Zambuzie River, and you're going to come back with a boatload of bargain-friggin'-zinie-friggin'-zinies! No-one leaves here empty-handed. In fact some of yous'll need help.

Some of the nervous people are making for the door, afraid they will get locked in. DERMOT *appears at the end of the hall.*

EDDIE: All right, lock the doors, they're comin' in the windows!

DERMOT walks through the crowd collecting fifty pounds from all the remaining customers. EDDIE *collects some money up towards the stage end.* DERMOT *comes up onto the stage and drops the lot into a suitcase at the side of the stage.* EDDIE *does likewise. They both look in at the money.*

EDDIE: I tell yeh, if I didn't have to hand this over every day I'd be laughin' altogether so I would. I swear to God it breaks me bloody heart, boy!

DERMOT (*turns, looks at* EDDIE): Yeah?

EDDIE *looks into* DERMOT's *anxious eyes as he waits for the cream-off.* EDDIE *peels off fifty pounds and slips it to him, doing likewise for himself.*

EDDIE: Say nothin' to your uncle about this.

DERMOT: What do yeh take me for, eh?

EDDIE: Say nothin' to no-one about it!

DERMOT: All right, stop fussin' will yeh?

EDDIE (*going back to work*): All right, Trojan Eddie has come to town! (DERMOT *lips the line.*)

EXT. SCRAPYARD. DAY.

EDDIE *and* DERMOT *drive into the yard in a van.* GINGER *and* REG *are busy unloading a truck-load of washbasins and sinks etc.* EDDIE *and* DERMOT *get out.*

EDDIE *is clearly uneasy in these surroundings.* GINGER *approaches.* EDDIE *nods to* REG.

GINGER: Well what do yeh know, the workers are home from the hills!

DERMOT (*smiling*): How's it goin', boys?

> EDDIE *goes to the old store-room and tries the door. It is locked.*

EDDIE (*to* GINGER): We need to load up for next week.

GINGER: Yeah?

REG: Here you go.

> REG *takes the bunch of keys from* GINGER's *coat pocket which is hanging on the side of the truck and he throws them to* GINGER. GINGER *catches them and holds them out to* EDDIE. EDDIE *does not stir. He knows* GINGER *too well.* GINGER *is forever hitting and hurting and play-acting with* EDDIE. GINGER *laughs and opens the door himself.*

> EDDIE *steps inside. When he is on the threshold* GINGER *kicks him in the back and drives him into the store-room. Then he quickly bangs shut the door and locks it.*

INT. STORE-ROOM. DAY.

EDDIE *is locked inside the dark store-room. He can hear the others laughing outside. He sighs and reaches for the light switch. He finds it and turns on the light.*

He looks around at the stacked up store-room which is packed up with cassette players and portable phones and razors and boxes galore, all the stuff that he sells. He ducks under a beam, turns and sits down on a box. DERMOT *opens the door and enters.*

EDDIE (*to* DERMOT): Start loadin' her up there, will yeh. Take as many of those what-do-you-call-its as you can find.

> EDDIE *walks towards boxes.* GINGER *is standing in the doorway.*

GINGER (*to* EDDIE): Since when did you start giving orders around here, eh, boy? Huh?

> Where's the money?

> EDDIE *steps to* GINGER – GINGER *steps aside as* EDDIE *exits and goes to the van.* EDDIE *takes the case from the van and steps to him.* GINGER *snatches it and walks away.*

EDDIE (*to* GINGER): Is your Da around?

GINGER: He's up above, why?

EDDIE: Just wonderin'.

GINGER: Yeah, well, don't.

> GINGER *goes up the stairs to the office.* EDDIE *watches him go, looking up at the office window to see* JOHN *staring down on him.* EDDIE *turns away from his earnest eyes only to find himself gazing into* CAROL's *lonely face as she stands in the doorway of the little house across the way.* DERMOT *comes out of the store-room with his arms full of merchandise which he brings to the van.*

DERMOT: All right, Eddie?

EDDIE: What? Yeah.

> EDDIE *goes into the store.* DERMOT *smiles and winks at* CAROL *and then he follows* EDDIE *into the store.* CAROL's *lonely face.*

INT. BAR. EVENING.

EDDIE *enters* MATT's *dark public house.* MATT *the barman is behind the counter reading the evening newspaper.*

EDDIE (*to* MATT): Hi, Matt.

MATT *gestures to reveal* RAYMIE *leaning over a pool table.* EDDIE *walks over to him.*

RAYMIE (*to* EDDIE): Had a visit from the Powers this morning, looking for their money. I got this big antique wardrobe off them a couple of weeks ago there.

EDDIE: So give it back to them.

RAYMIE: I've already sold it, sure, and spent the money. . . . Well, I mean, I have to live!

To tell you the truth, I think Ginger just fancies taking a smack at me over that other thing.

EDDIE: I mean, how many times do I have to tell yeh? She's trouble!

RAYMIE: But sure nothin' really happened anyway, like, yeh know.

EDDIE: Just stay away from her altogether.

RAYMIE: I'll be all right. I'll wangle me way out of it all right. Fuckin' pricks.

So, how's business?

EDDIE: All right.

RAYMIE: Yeah?

EDDIE: Yeah.

RAYMIE: Do yeh miss me? (EDDIE *sort of shrugs.*) Huh? (RAYMIE *taps* EDDIE's *arm with cue.*) Hey, we were a good team, mate! Until that other little shit came along.

EDDIE: Dermot's all right!

RAYMIE: What do yeh mean he's all right? He's hard set to count to ten.

EDDIE: He can count all right.

RAYMIE: Huh?

We should break away on our own anyway. Start up our own little outfit.

EDDIE *indicates a lack of money.*

12

RAYMIE: We could pull off a bit of a job. . . . Why not? I
still have the Balaclavas. All right, I know the last job
didn't go so well for you and all . . .

EDDIE: Yeah, like twelve months.

RAYMIE: Yeah, I know, but I mean to say, these things
happen, like, yeh know. I mean, where else are we goin'
to get it? I mean, it's not goin' to fall from the sky or
anythin' is it?

EXT. GRAVEYARD. DAY.
*A multitude of people are gathered in the local cemetery for the
annual patron.*

*A brass band is playing somewhere in the distance and a
PRIEST's voice can be heard over the loudspeakers. We see
EDDIE and his family among the throng – his MOTHER and
two DAUGHTERS.*

*A few graves up RAYMIE can be seen, blessing himself.
Across the way JOHN POWER, DERMOT, GINGER and
CAROL mingle with a host of travellers. RAYMIE smiles
nervously at CAROL as she looks his way.*

PRIEST: We are gathered here today to remember our
deceased relatives, friends and loved ones, and to
honour their memory with our presence and our
prayers. And as I look around me here today and see the
beautiful resting places – the flowers and the urns and
the beautiful well-kept graves, I can't help but think
how fortunate we are to be living in a land where the
dead are not forgotten, and where the souls of our dead
are not left to be abandoned to the abyss.

We still believe, thank God, in the Communion of the
Saints, in the forgiveness of sins and in the Resurrection
of the dead and the life of the world to come . . .

13

JOHN POWER *is standing beside a grave amidst the travellers,* GINGER *and* CAROL *close by.* GERRY *and his wife* ROSY *make their way over to him.*

GERRY (*blessing himself*): Poor old Kitty. God be good to her, huh! Yeh keep the grave lovely anyway, John, fair play to you.

JOHN (*to* GERRY): Hm?

GERRY: The grave – yeh keep it lovely, John.

JOHN: Well, it's the least I could do. She was a great wife and a very good mother.

GINGER (*to* CAROL): Come on.

GERRY (*over, to* JOHN): She was that all right.

JOHN *stares down at the grave.*

GERRY (*to* KATHLEEN, *approaching*): Kathleen? This is my eldest girl now, John.

KATHLEEN (*to* GERRY): What?

GERRY: Did you say a prayer for poor auld Kitty?

KATHLEEN: Yeah.

JOHN *has not seen her since she was a girl and now he cannot believe his eyes. He is enchanted by her beauty. She looks into his sad eyes before she moves away.* JOHN's *eyes follow her everywhere as she weaves her way through the throng of travellers.*

In another part of the graveyard are EDDIE *and his family. The brass band approaches.* BETTY *arrives. She kisses* EDDIE *and links her arm into his.*

MOTHER: Here's Betty. How are yeh, Betty?

GIRLS: How are yeh, Betty?

BETTY: How are yeh, lads? I see the lads are here in force anyway. (*The hundreds of travellers across the way.*)

MOTHER: Every year boy, without fail!

BETTY: It's a wonder he's not over there with them.

MOTHER: It's a great wonder to me he isn't then.

EDDIE *nods and turns to look at* RAYMIE *who is close by now, larking with the children.* BETTY *watches* EDDIE *lovingly.* MOTHER *sees the love in her eyes and smiles sadly, hoping for the best.*

BETTY: I'm just nipping across to say a prayer for Doreen.

MOTHER: I'm goin' to tell you one thing, son, but you fell on your feet the day yeh met her.

EDDIE: Yeh reckon?

MOTHER: Yeah. I do.

RAYMIE: She's too good for him though, Madge, ain't she? Huh?

MOTHER: She's not one bit too good for him at all. He comes from a respectable family and don't you forget it.

EDDIE: Oon the Ma, boy!

RAYMIE: Fair play to yeh, Madge.

KATHLEEN *walks through the graveyard talking to the travellers. She stops and talks to a young man. He takes her hand and leads her behind monuments.* JOHN *is still watching her.*

DERMOT *steps over to* JOHN *and taps his arm.*

DERMOT (*to* JOHN): How are yeh, John?

JOHN: Yeah. Dermot, who's that there?

DERMOT: Huh?

JOHN: The fella talking to Gerry's daughter.

DERMOT: Oh, that's, um, Patsy McDonagh.

JOHN (*to himself*): Patsy McDonagh.

EXT. TRAVELLERS' HALTING SITE. VERY EARLY MORNING.
A cluster of caravans nestle in the middle of an open field. Ponies, horses and goats are grazing all around and a few mangy dogs are prowling around the scrap heaps. KATHLEEN *approaches with two buckets of water. Patsy McDonagh comes towards her, barefoot.*

PATSY: Kathleen! Give us those buckets will yeh.

15

He gives her a hand to carry the buckets and as they
approach they converse happily, clearly at ease with each
other.

KATHLEEN: What are yeh doin' out here with no shoes on
    yeh?

PATSY: Ah, yeh know me, a hardy snipe.

KATHLEEN: Yeah, well, yeh won't be so hardy when you've
    a big, dirty piece of glass up your foot.

PATSY: Stop fussin' will yeh. . . . Who were yeh smilin' at
    anyway?

KATHLEEN: When?

PATSY: Comin' across the field.

KATHLEEN: Ah, I was just thinkin' about a song I heard in
    the pub last night.

PATSY: What was the name of it?

KATHLEEN: I don't know. Something angel or something. I
    can't think of it now.

INT. BEDROOM. EARLY MORNING.
EDDIE *and* BETTY *in bed.* EDDIE *looks at the alarm clock. He*
rises and begins to dress quietly. BETTY *sighs and turns over*
sleepily. EDDIE *bends to kiss her. She takes his hand and kisses*
it.

EXT. STREET. EARLY MORNING.
EDDIE *comes out onto the silent, empty street and slips*
stealthily across the road to his own house, three or four houses
down. The milkman disappears into the next street.

INT. HOUSE. EARLY MORNING.
EDDIE *enters through the front door. He tiptoes up the stairs,*
stopping on the landing to gaze in at his youngest girl asleep in

16

*her bed. He then peeps into the box-room where his oldest girl is
sleeping. He goes into his own bedroom to get ready for work.*

EXT. HALTING SITE. DAY.
*A dirt road leading up to a travellers' halting site – two or three
caravans, children playing, a bonfire burning, goats and dogs
prowling etc.* GERRY, *stripped to the waist, punches a big
sandbag, dancing around like a prize fighter.* ROSY, *his wife,
watches him from the doorway of an ornate caravan.*

INT. EDDIE'S VAN. DAY.
EDDIE *is sitting in his stationary van. He is talking on his
mobile phone.*

EDDIE (*into phone*): Right, see yeh later.
     EDDIE *hangs up as* DERMOT *opens the van door and*
     KATHLEEN *climbs in.* EDDIE *seems bewildered.*
DERMOT (*getting in*): Let's go.
EDDIE: Yeah? This is it?
     DERMOT *nods.*
DERMOT (*to* EDDIE): Yeah.
     The van drives off down the dirt road. Back to GERRY
     and ROSY *as they stand watching the van driving away.*
GERRY (*to* ROSY *o.s.*): Could be a good match for her, Rosy,
     yeh know.
ROSY: It's not right Gerry. I don't care what yeh say. She's
     too young and he's too old. I don't care what yeh say.
     *The family are waving, the children running along beside
     the van. They pass the* MCDONAGH *halting site on the
     way.* PATSY *is standing in the doorway of a caravan.*
     KATHLEEN *smiles tenderly at him as they pass.*

17

EXT. SCRAPYARD. DAY.

CAROL (*to* GINGER): So, what time? I need to know if I'm making your dinner.

GINGER: Just have the dinner ready. Right? I want it better than that heap of shite you gave me for a breakfast.

CAROL: There's no point in eating it so, is there?

GINGER: Fucking dogs wouldn't eat it. Here's my father. I've got to go.

JOHN *walks down the steps from his office and across the yard.* GINGER *opens car door.*

INT. VAN. EVENING.

EDDIE *and* DERMOT *and* KATHLEEN *are travelling in the van.* DERMOT *and* KATHLEEN *are sort of snuggled into each other as they sing along to a tape.*

KATHLEEN/DERMOT (*singing*): Oh, the prickly bush/ It fills my heart full of sore/ And if ever I get away from that bush/ I'll never get caught any more . . .

DERMOT (*to* EDDIE): Her Da is a bare-knuckle boxer, yeh know.

EDDIE: Yeah?

KATHLEEN: Yeah, he'd bate yeh just for lookin' at me.

EDDIE: I wasn't lookin' at yeh.

EXT. COUNTRY ROAD. DAY.

EDDIE's *van travelling along the road.* EDDIE, DERMOT *and* KATHLEEN *seen through windscreen.*

DERMOT: Hey Eddie, tell her about yourself and Raymie. Himself and Raymie knocked off a post office one time yeh know. Balaclavas and a toy gun. They got away with it an' all, only for Eddie bought himself a car, (*Laughs.*)

18

which looked kind of suspicious.

(*To* EDDIE.) What did yeh get, Eddie – twelve months?

(*To* KATHLEEN.) They gave him a year because he wouldn't grass on the other fella . . .

EDDIE *is a little piqued as* KATHLEEN *looks disdainfully into his eyes.*

DERMOT: But sure, as the cowboy said to the horse, 'why the long face?' Do yeh get it? Why the long face? *Laughter.*

EDDIE: Jaysus! Let me out of here, will yeh?

DERMOT *throws back his head and laughs as he looks into her eyes. Then he turns and his smiling face is shadowed when he spies the Mercedes parked in a lane just up ahead.* JOHN POWER *is standing beside it and there is something chilling about his appearance there. All three turn serious as the van pulls in.*

EXT. WOODLANDS. DAY.

JOHN *and* KATHLEEN *are climbing down a steep hill to a beautiful clearing in the woods beside a river.*

JOHN: We pulled our little barrel-topped wagon down that hill there. Right across here – let the horses off and this is where we pitched our camp. (*Sighs.*) Yeah, we were fine and snug here. Fresh water and look – lashings of firewood for the fire. Meself and me little sister Bridget were in our alley altogether – running here through the woods. (*To* KATHLEEN.) See those rocks? There, we used to be climbing up those rocks.

I started rambling into town, knocking around with a few local lads, old billiard halls and that. Then my sister Bridget met a settled boy and – ran off and got married.

Dermot's mother and father.

That same summer the family thought it was time to move on but I refused to go. Me Dada was terrible disappointed I think. Ragin' with himself really, for dawdlin' too long in the one spot. And he tried – to persuade me to go along with them, (*sighs*) but I didn't. Sure my mind was made up. And they went off without me. I never took to the road again. Me wings were sort of clipped, I suppose.

KATHLEEN (*coming close to him*): But you married a traveller?

JOHN: Aye. I married a traveller – old Kitty. The Lord be good to her.
Pause.

KATHLEEN: I don't like the road, meself. When I get married I'm wanting to live in a house. Bit of an orchard out the back and a swing for the children and all. (*Looking at* JOHN.) People think that travellers don't like beautiful things, but we do. And, they think that we don't feel the cold as well, but that's not true either.
She moves towards the river, lying down on a big boulder, drags a leaf through the rushing water below her. JOHN *watches, sitting on the riverbank, bewitched by her.*
I love the feel of fresh water. The sound of it. And the wonder of it. Where it comes from and where it's goin' to and all.

JOHN: It's a fairly powerful thing all right. I learnt to swim in there yeh know. (*Points to river.* KATHLEEN *turns to look.*) It was a case of having to. I fell in one day and before I knew it I was – yeh know – sort of swimming.
KATHLEEN *laughs.* JOHN *smiles. He runs out of words. She looks deep into his eyes. He grows tender. Slight pause.*

JOHN: But, sure, everyone likes beautiful things.
Awkward pause.

KATHLEEN (*suddenly sitting up straight*): I think I'll go for a bit of a swim meself.

21

JOHN (*whispers*): What? Jaysus Kathleen.

KATHLEEN (*v/o*): What? Keep an eye out won't yeh. Tell me if anyone's coming.

JOHN: What?

KATHLEEN (*v/o to* JOHN): Go on with yeh!

JOHN stands up. She has her back to him and her young naked body spawns a terrible sadness to rise inside of him.

JOHN (*to* KATHLEEN): Jaysus, Kathleen. I'd rather you wouldn't.

Just before she plunges she turns and smiles at him and then she dives and as he watches her swim away from him he longs to be young again. He retreats behind the rock again, a little ashamed and a little frightened.

In the background, DERMOT's *silhouette. He stares at* KATHLEEN *as she swims.*

INT. VAN. NIGHT.

EDDIE, DERMOT *and* KATHLEEN *are travelling in the van up the dirt road to the halting site.* DERMOT *is sulking.* KATHLEEN *wondering about it.* EDDIE *feels slightly uneasy.*

DERMOT (*o.s.*): Pull in here.

EDDIE (*to* DERMOT): What?

DERMOT: I'll walk her across the field.

EDDIE: What for?

DERMOT: In case we wake the children.

EDDIE *pulls over.* DERMOT *and* KATHLEEN *get out and disappear into the darkness.* EDDIE's *worried face.*

EXT. FIELD. NIGHT.

DERMOT *and* KATHLEEN *are walking across the field.*

KATHLEEN: What do yeh mean I was actin' the Mary Magdalen?

DERMOT: Stripping in front of that old man! You think he's
going to respect yeh after that! Do me a favour will yeh!

KATHLEEN: He does so respect me. And for your
information he's wantin' to marry me.

DERMOT: Yeah? And do yeh want to know why? Did yeh
even ask yourself why? Well, I'll tell yeh why, because
yeh remind him of his wife, me Auntie Kitty, that's
why. So yeh needn't bother your arse flatterin' yourself
at all there, girl.

INT. VAN. NIGHT.

A TRAVELLER *peers through window. Bangs on window, turns,
he and other* TRAVELLERS *walk off.* EDDIE *sits unmoving,
watches them, nervous.*

MAN (*in Shelta – the travellers' secret language*): A townie at
the wheel, lads.

SECOND MAN (*over*): Yeah.
They walk off, away from van.

EXT. FIELD. NIGHT.
KATHLEEN *stops, turns to* DERMOT.

KATHLEEN: I'm me. Meself. No-one else and I won't be
lumped with anyone else either. Not by you, or him, or
anyone!

DERMOT *moves towards her. She steps back to keep him
at bay then she sort of hisses and holds up her hand as if to
put a hex on someone.*

DERMOT: Whoa! Take it easy. Take it easy now. (DERMOT
*slowly reaches in for her hand and gently lowers it to her
side.*) There's no need for that now. Take it easy.

He caresses her hair and then her face. He kisses her
gently. She responds, tenderly at first and then
passionately.

INT. VAN. NIGHT.

EDDIE *waits in the van, impatiently.*

   Soon DERMOT *appears out of the darkness and climbs into*
the van.

EDDIE: What are you tryin' to do, get the two of us killed or
    somethin'?

DERMOT: Look, stop worryin' will yeh, nothin' happened.

EDDIE: Nothin' happened! In an hour and a half and nothin'
    happened.

DERMOT: Yeah well, it's done now. It's over, forget it, come
    on. Let's go.

EDDIE: What do yeh mean, forget it?

DERMOT: Forget it. Come on, let's go.

EDDIE (*shouts*): Just a minute, pal! I've been waitin' here for
    you for an hour and a fuckin' half, mate. An hour and a
    half!

DERMOT: So what? Do yeh want to do somethin' about it or
    somethin', huh? Come on! Come on, do somethin'
    about it, huh?

   DERMOT *opens the door and gets out.*

DERMOT: Come on! . . .

   EDDIE *stares at him, shakes his head. Pause.* EDDIE *sighs*
   and starts up the van. DERMOT *climbs back inside.*

EDDIE: I don't know.

   They drive away in silence. EDDIE *shakes his head and*
   sighs. DERMOT *is a little ashamed of his outburst.*

EDDIE: I only hope she was worth it, that's all I hope.

INT. CARAVAN. NIGHT.

KATHLEEN *undresses. She is surrounded by a heap of sleeping brothers and sisters. She sighs at her circumstances, moves over to the bed.*

LITTLE GIRL *(whispers)*: What are yeh doin' Kathleen?
KATHLEEN: Nothin'. Go back to sleep.

INT. HOUSE. NIGHT.

EDDIE *is coming through his own front door.* MOTHER *comes to meet him in the hall, a worried look on her face. The two* GIRLS *are huddled together in the kitchen doorway, puzzled looking.*

MOTHER: She's back Eddie. Tell her to go. You're better off
    without her altogether. She's no bloody good, that one.
    Such a night as I'm after puttin' in with her here!
    EDDIE *goes towards the living room, fondling the children*
    lovingly as he moves. His heart is thumping as he longs to
    see her again.

INT. LIVING ROOM. EVENING.

SHIRLEY *is sitting in the living room in front of the television. She turns to look at* EDDIE *as he enters.*

EDDIE: How are yeh, Shirley?
SHIRLEY: How are yeh?
    MOTHER *enters, putting on her coat, a face of vengeance*
    on her.
MOTHER: I'm off now, Eddie. I'm wantin' to go home and
    get ready for me late-night bingo.
    EDDIE *mumbles, reaches into his pocket and takes out*
    some money. He peels off a few notes and gives them to her.
MOTHER *(whispers)*: Thanks, Eddie.

She touches his face tenderly. Then she throws SHIRLEY *a dirty look and leaves.*

SHIRLEY: Look, if there's a problem, just say so.

EDDIE: There's no problem.

SHIRLEY: Okay. I mean, I still have a stake in this house, yeh know. A big stake. So if there's a problem . . .

EDDIE: There's no problem.

SHIRLEY: Right.

    EDDIE *looks at the bewildered children.*

EDDIE: Go ahead upstairs, lads, will yous. Good girls. (*They obey,* EDDIE *closes the door after them.*)

    So, what happened?

SHIRLEY: What do yeh mean, what happened? Nothin' happened. (*Looks down, shrugs.*) I just need a place to stay for a little while, that's all. I mean, if it's too much to ask that I can come and stay in me own house, well!

EDDIE: Look, I told yeh before, you can come back any time. I told yeh that. Yeh know that. You're still my wife and their mother. There's always room for you here. You know that.

SHIRLEY (*raising her eyebrows*): Yeah?

EDDIE: Yeah. I mean . . .

SHIRLEY: Yeah, well I sort of heard somethin' to the contrary, Eddie, like, yeh know.

    EDDIE *is a little embarrassed.*

SHIRLEY: Anyway, Eddie, don't worry about it. I won't be stoppin' too long. I'll stick me bags into the little box room.

    She rises. EDDIE *sighs.*

EDDIE: Um . . .

SHIRLEY: What?

    She turns to look at him.

EDDIE: Nothin'. I just promised Jenny that she could have her own room, that's all. It's all right. It don't matter.

SHIRLEY *moves towards the stairs and starts to walk up.*

SHIRLEY (*stopping on the stairs*): And where's the clock?
(*There is a mark of the old clock on the wall.*) Don't tell
me, the price was right. Right? (SHIRLEY *sighs and
walks upstairs.*)
EDDIE's *sad bewildered face.*

EXT. STREET. MORNING.
Sunday morning. Bells ringing. EDDIE *and the two* GIRLS *are
walking down the street in their Sunday clothes. They walk
down steps that lead them to* BETTY's *house.*

INT. HOUSE. DAY.
EDDIE *and* BETTY *in living room –* GIRLS *play in the garden
in background.*

BETTY: How long is she stayin' for?

EDDIE: I don't know. A couple of weeks, somethin' like
that. I told her out straight, I'm not having it. I mean to
say, the children are upset enough without all that.

BETTY: Well, maybe yeh have to put your foot down with
her this time, Eddie. I mean, what are people goin' to
think, like? Her comin' back whenever she feels like it.
Anyway . . .
(BETTY *turns and goes to the couch. From under the
cushions she takes out a couple of travel brochures.*)

BETTY: Meself and your mother were droolin' over these
the other day. Yeh should have seen her, Eddie.
'Imagine,' says she, 'A holiday in the sun!' What do yeh
think?

EDDIE: I don't know. Show us.
She gives him a brochure.

BETTY: I mean, I don't mind meself, as long as there's
sunshine.

28

EDDIE *half-heartedly thumbs his way through the brochure.*

EDDIE: How much?

BETTY: Well, if we were to book it now, we'd get it under a thousand for the lot of us. And that's not bad. I mean, we'd be goin' in peak time, yeh know. Nine seventy-five.

EDDIE: A thousand more or less.

BETTY: But sure, I'll go halves with yeh.

EDDIE: Ah, no, I wouldn't expect that.

BETTY: No, I've me money saved and all. We could have a great time out there sure! The kids! And your mother!

EDDIE: I was half thinkin' of branchin' out on me own, like, yeh know, and a thousand could go a long way. (*He looks down.*)

BETTY: Well, at least think about it.

EDDIE: Oh yeah, I mean . . . I'll definitely think about it.

EDDIE *turns away from* BETTY's *disappointed face.*

EXT. STREET. DAY.

EDDIE, BETTY *and the two* GIRLS *are walking down the street. The Mercedes pulls in beside them.* GINGER *is driving,* JOHN *in the back seat.*

GINGER: Da wants a word with yeh.

EDDIE: What?

GINGER: Get in.

EDDIE *sighs and turns to* BETTY.

EDDIE: Take the lads up home for me, Betty, will yeh.

BETTY: Yeah, right.

GIRLS: Bye, Daddy.

EDDIE: Yeah, right lads. See yeh later on, eh?

BETTY *takes the children away.* EDDIE *reluctantly gets into the back with* JOHN.

INT. CAR. DAY.

EDDIE *is in the back of the car with* JOHN.

JOHN (*to* GINGER): Ginger, get us a paper.

> (GINGER *gets out and crosses the street to a vendor.*
> *Silence.*) You didn't leave Dermot alone with the girl at
> any time last night, did yeh?

EDDIE: No.

JOHN: Did yeh leave her to the door?

EDDIE: No, we dropped her at the end of the field.

JOHN: What did yeh do that for?

EDDIE: We didn't want to wake the children.

JOHN: Was that Dermot's idea?

EDDIE: No, I don't think so.

JOHN: What?

EDDIE: No, it was, er . . . what-do-you-call-it . . . I don't
> know. All our ideas, like.

JOHN: All your ideas?

EDDIE: Yeah, more or less.

JOHN: More or less?

EDDIE: Yeah.

JOHN: Well, which was it?

EDDIE: Huh?

JOHN: I mean, was it more or less . . .

> (JOHN *looks at* EDDIE. EDDIE *looks at* JOHN.
> *Silence.*) Why then, how come she didn't get home until
> after half-eleven?

EDDIE: Don't know. She must have went somewhere
else.

JOHN: Oh! (*Pause.*) Where?

> EDDIE *shrugs nervously.* JOHN *looks into his eyes.*
> GINGER *is returning.*

JOHN: Show me.

EXT. TRAVELLERS' HALTING SITE. DAY.
JOHN's *car arrives at site. Children playing.* PATSY
MCDONAGH *is leaning over a car engine.*

GINGER (*to* PATSY): Patsy McDonagh? Yeh whoreman,
    yeh!

EXT. FIELD. DAY.
EDDIE *is standing in field. Soon a young man comes running
towards him, terror in his eyes.* GINGER *is running after him.
This is young* PATSY MCDONAGH.

GINGER (*calling out to* EDDIE): Stop him. Stop him, yeh
    fuckin' prick, yeh, stop him or I'll bate yeh, good-
    lookin'.
    EDDIE *makes a dive for* PATSY *and they wrestle each
    other to the ground.* GINGER *is soon on top of them and*
    EDDIE *is forced to roll out of the way, away from*
    GINGER's *vicious kicks and punches. In fact in the melee*
    EDDIE's *mouth is cut.*
EDDIE (*shouts*): Jaysus, Ginger. Ginger, come on.
GINGER (*to* EDDIE): Oh, for fuck's sake!
    EDDIE *pulls* GINGER *away from* PATSY. PATSY *turns
    and runs.*
GINGER (*to* EDDIE): Fuck off, you.
    (PATSY *runs through marsh, falls.* GINGER *hurries
    through marsh to* PATSY.)
GINGER: You'd never think a grown man could drown in
    three or four inches of water would yeh? You can,
    watch!
    GINGER *holds the young man's head down into the marsh,
    one foot pushing down on the young man's back.* EDDIE
    watches on in horror as the young man struggles.

EDDIE (*shouts*): What are yeh tryin' to do, kill the chap or somethin'? Jesus! I mean, what did he do anyway?

JOHN *arrives.*

GINGER (*to* PATSY): You were told, weren't yeh? (*Shouts.*) Huh? You were told, weren't yeh? You bastard!

GINGER *pulls* PATSY *to his knees.* JOHN *walks through marsh to them.*

JOHN (*to* GINGER): Bring him here.

GINGER *drags* PATSY *to* JOHN'*s feet.*

JOHN (*throwing money into his face*): Here, take this now. Then get out of here. Take the Mail Boat to London tonight. Don't ever come back here again, or I'll kill yeh.

They leave. EDDIE *pauses to look down with pity on the poor travelling boy. Then* EDDIE *turns and follows the others.*

PATSY MCDONAGH: Why London? I don't know no-one over there.

GINGER (*laughs*): You don't know no-one over there, d'you know. Yeh bastard, yeh. (EDDIE *catches up on them.* GINGER *rounds on him.*) You're goin' to get it from me one of these days, boy, yeh know that?

EDDIE *stops in his tracks.* GINGER *moves on.* EDDIE *looks back at the young man in the distance, still down on all fours as he wonders why he was beaten up. He stands up, stumbles.*

INT. BAR. NIGHT.

MATT'*s bar. A close-up of* JOHN POWER'*s face as he sings, drunkenly. The camera pulls back and we see* EDDIE *standing beside him at the counter.* MATT *the barman looks a little annoyed with* EDDIE *for bringing them in here.* GINGER *is over at the jukebox, looking at his own wolf-like reflection.* CAROL *is sitting like an outcast at a nearby table.*

At one stage RAYMIE *looks into the bar, sees the* POWERS *and sensing trouble he scarpers.* EDDIE *picks up a few drinks from the counter and takes them across to* GINGER *and* CAROL.

CAROL (*to* EDDIE): I think I made a big mistake Eddie, gettin' involved with these people.

EDDIE: We all make our own beds to lie in them.

CAROL: Yeah, I know, but . . . all the same.

    EDDIE *goes back to the bar.*

JOHN (*looking into* EDDIE*'s face*): Yeh know, every time I look at you I feel like shoutin' 'man overboard'.

EDDIE: I'm all right.

JOHN: What?

EDDIE: Nothin'.

JOHN: What did yeh say, I said?

EDDIE: I said, I'm all right.

JOHN (*laughs*): Sure you're goin' down with the ship, boy. I feel like throwin' you a life-jacket or somethin'. (JOHN *leans over, rests his arm on bar and holds up his fist.*) Do you see that fist? Go on, take a look at that fist. Do yeh see those rings? Do yeh? They're my father's rings. I broke a fella's jaw with that fist one night. And another night, another night, I broke a fella's nose. (JOHN *imitates head-butting* EDDIE.) Like that. Like that. (*Whispers.*) Did yeh ever hear the sound of a nose breakin'? No? It's a sore sound. Yeh know? (JOHN *stands, removes jacket, rips open shirtsleeve, points to his arm.*) Do you see that scar? Do yeh see it, do yeh? One night in a pub brawl a fella bit me there. He buried his teeth into me like a wolf. And then, he grabbed me by the balls, and squeezed until me nose bled. I won that fight. I won all those fights. (*Shouts.*) I won every fight I ever fought. Do yeh know what I mean, like? Ever!

34

MATT *is disdainfully clearing and wiping the counter around them.*

JOHN: What? (*Shouts.*) What? What?

MATT: What not!

JOHN (*to* MATT): Listen here, you. You fuck off, mate.

MATT: What nothin'.

JOHN: I said, fuck off, mate.

With a sweep of his hand he knocks all the glasses and bottles from the counter. GINGER *moves closer, poised for a fight.*

MATT: All right Mister Power, take it easy now, take it easy.

JOHN (*shouts*): Take it easy. That's what you're always saying to me, is take it easy! What do yeh take me for? Hah? Take it easy! That's what he does. He takes it easy. (*Points at* EDDIE.) D'yeh think I want to end up like him? Do yeh? He's a peasant. A buffer. But I'm a King. And a King needs a Queen . . . (*He steps back to view the entire bar.*) You people, you haven't a clue! No idea. None. When my family – Dada and my mam came in . . . You've no idea. (*Shouts.*) None whatsoever. None. (*Turns and walks towards door. To man in bar.*) Get out of my fucking way! (*Man moves,* JOHN *turns to* GINGER.) Come on, Ginger.

JOHN *leaves,* GINGER *follows. As he reaches door he turns, looks at* CAROL.

GINGER (*to* CAROL): Fuck off home, you! (*Exits.*)

EDDIE: I'm sorry about that, Matt.

MATT: Why did yeh bring them in here in the first place, for Christ's sake. Jaysus Christ – I don't know.

EXT. STREET. NIGHT.

EDDIE *is out on the street. He stands to watch* JOHN *and* GINGER *stagger away from him on the far side.* EDDIE's *face in the shadows.*

JOHN (*shouts o.s.*): You're a fucking buffer.

INT. EDDIE'S HOUSE. NIGHT.
EDDIE *arrives home.* SHIRLEY *is asleep on sofa in front of the telly.* EDDIE *watches her, a T.V. show on in the background. He switches off the T.V.* SHIRLEY *turns, looks at him. She sits up.*

EDDIE: Are the girls in bed?

SHIRLEY: Yeah. You're overworked, Eddie, and yeh know what they say about that, don't yeh?

EDDIE: Ah, no. I wasn't workin'. I just got roped into somethin', that's all.

SHIRLEY: Still the good little boy yeh used to be, huh? Comin' when you're called!

EDDIE: Yeah well, not for much longer, I can tell yeh.

SHIRLEY: Yeah?

EDDIE: I'm thinkin' about branchin' out on me own, yeh know. I mean, you'd be better off with a sort of a permanent place downtown somewhere. Let them come to me for a change.

SHIRLEY: Yeah, but it all takes money though, don't it?

EDDIE: I'm startin' to get a few quid together now, like, yeh know. Cream a little bit off from the top now and then, like, yeh know. (*He smiles.*)

SHIRLEY: Before yeh know it you'll be takin' a holiday in the sun and everything.
Awkward pause. SHIRLEY *leans to him.*

SHIRLEY: So, tell me about this place then. I mean, do yeh have a particular place in mind and that?

EDDIE (*falling under her spell*): Yeah, there's a place downtown that's goin' for half-nothin', I believe. I mean, it'd take a bit of doin' up and that, but . . .

36

(*shrugs*) I mean, I don't need a palace or anything. Four
walls and a door and I'd make money.

SHIRLEY: I see, said the blind man. Trojan Eddie, huh?

EDDIE: Yeah – a little hat on me head and all!
They both chuckle.

SHIRLEY: Listen, Eddie, is there a spare key around
anywhere?

EDDIE: Huh? Yeah, out in the kitchen there – hangin' up on
the old yoke-me-bob out there . . .
SHIRLEY *disappears into the kitchen. She returns putting
on her coat.*

SHIRLEY: I'm goin' out for a while. Don't wait up for me.
She goes. EDDIE's *heart-broken face.*

EXT. SCRAPYARD. DAY.
A van arrives in the yard. KATHLEEN *and* GERRY *get out.
She looks around the yard. Everyone has stopped working.*
GINGER *and* REG, *and* CAROL *in the doorway polishing the
knockers.* JOHN *comes out onto the landing above. He gestures
for her to come up. Slowly she makes her way up to the office,
stopping on the landing to look out over the place like a queen
surveying her domain.* GERRY *is looking at her proudly.*
GINGER *looks a little hurt,* CAROL *a little jealous.* JOHN *and*
KATHLEEN *go into the office.*

INT. OFFICE. DAY.
KATHLEEN *looks around the office,* JOHN *looking on. She goes
to a curtain and draws it back to reveal a long narrow room
choc-a-bloc with antiques – old grandfather clocks and chaise
longues and old hat stands etc.*

JOHN: The house.
*She goes down through this room to stand at the window
which overlooks the house which has a little orchard out the*

*back. She grows tender as she watches it. He comes closer.
She looks at him and smiles, tears in her eyes. He grows
tender and falls to his knees, burying his head into her
body.*

JOHN (*whispers*): Oh, Kathleen! . . . Kathleen . . .

*She looks down at him and eventually she runs her fingers
through his hair. A close up on her face. Regal and proud.*

EXT. TRAVELLERS' HALTING SITE. MORNING.

*The Mercedes is parked outside the little cluster of caravans. It
is bedecked with ribbons and* EDDIE *is at the wheel. A crowd is
gathered around the car, women and children and a few of the*
MCDONAGH *family.* EDDIE *feels a little uneasy as he looks
from one face to another, especially when his gaze falls upon the
sad-eyed* PATSY MCDONAGH. KATHLEEN's *family are all
dressed in their good clothes and the people around them are
admiring them etc. And then the door opens and* KATHLEEN
appears in her wedding dress, her two sisters behind her (the
BRIDESMAIDS). *A delighted gasp goes all around the halting
site. Her mother is weeping as* GERRY *helps the bride into the
car and they drive away. A close up of* PATSY's *face as they
disappear.*

EXT. ORCHARD. DAY.

*Sharp cut to a little Irish showband playing and singing 'Old
Man Trouble'. The wedding is taking place in the orchard at
the back of* JOHN POWER's *house. Tables are laid out in the
open grounds and there is a big marquee in the background.*

*The guests are mainly travellers, all dressed in their garish
dresses and swanky suits. The band is mounted on a makeshift
stage and there is a wooden dance floor erected in the middle of
the orchard with a canopy overhead.*

We go from group to group – JOHN *and* KATHLEEN (*the*

38

bride and groom), DERMOT *and* GINGER *and* LADY CASH *sitting like a queen close to the main table as people come up to her to tell her their troubles etc.*

MAN: Ladies and gentlemen, the bride and groom!

JOHN *and* KATHLEEN *walk through marquee to dance floor. They dance and twirl as the guests look on.*

GERRY *and* ROSY *mingle proudly with the other guests and close to the bandstand* EDDIE*'s little suitcase is balanced haphazardly on a chair. As people pass it they throw money into it so that it is filling up steadily.* EDDIE *is working about the place, looking like a fish out of water. Out on the dance floor* RAYMIE *is jiving stylishly with* CAROL, *much to* EDDIE*'s chagrin.* GINGER *is watching from afar.*

Then EDDIE *spies* SHIRLEY *in the crowd and his heart soars when he sees her only to sink again as he realises that she is with* GINGER.

EDDIE *goes across to* RAYMIE. *He puts his arm around him and leads him away from the dance floor.*

EDDIE: Hey, what are yeh doin'?

RAYMIE: What do yeh mean? I'm dancin'! Dancin'!

EDDIE: You're supposed to be watchin' the cars!

RAYMIE: But sure, the cars are out there.

EDDIE: I know. That's the point. You're supposed to be watchin' them.

RAYMIE: I mean, what's the problem, anyway. The girl asked me to dance. What am I supposed to do? Refuse her? I mean, I feel sort of sorry for her – gettin' mixed up with this crowd.

EDDIE: She made her bed.

RAYMIE: Yeah, I know all that but, nevertheless . . .

EDDIE: Anyway, you're gettin' paid to watch the cars, not to dance with her. So watch the cars!

RAYMIE: What's wrong with you? Huh? I mean, this is just a what-do-you-call-it . . . I mean – What's wrong with you?

EDDIE (*shouts*): Are you going to watch the cars, or not?

RAYMIE (*shouts*): No, I'm not . . . Watch the cars!

EDDIE: Where are yeh goin'? If you go, I'm not payin' yeh. I'm warnin' yeh, Raymie, I'm not payin' yeh.

RAYMIE (*heading out the gate*): Yeah, yeah, yeah. . . . Watch the cars! What's wrong with you! (*He waves him away.*)
EDDIE *watches him go, turning to see* SHIRLEY *across the way talking to* GINGER. SHIRLEY *laughs as* GINGER *leads her away. She looks over her shoulder into* EDDIE's *sad eyes.* GINGER *leads her into the house, closing the door after them.* EDDIE *stands looking at the closed door.*

INT. KITCHEN. DAY.
EDDIE *is having a cup of tea in* BETTY's *house. The wedding sounds like a jamboree in the distance.*

BETTY (*a little worried about him*): Do yeh have to go back?

EDDIE: Yeah, I have to be there in case anyone needs a lift home, yeh know.

BETTY: So, did she look good?

EDDIE: Who?

BETTY: The bride.

EDDIE: Oh yeah. She looked grand. Lovely.

BETTY: So, who was there, all?

EDDIE: Oh, I don't know. Sure they came from near and far, like, yeh know.

BETTY: Yeah? Packed huh?

EDDIE: Yeah.

BETTY: So, who was there from near?

EDDIE: No-one you'd know. I mean, they were all, what-do-you-call-it, like, yeh know . . .

BETTY: Yeah? No, it's just that I thought I saw Shirley goin'
in there at one stage.

EDDIE: Yeah? When was that?

BETTY: Not so long ago.

EDDIE: Well, if yeh did, she's gatecrashin' then. . . . When
was it?

BETTY: I don't know, not too long ago.

EDDIE: All dressed up?

BETTY *nods*.

BETTY: Yeh didn't see her there then, no? (EDDIE *shakes his
head*.)

EDDIE: Look, she's not invited or anythin', if that's what
you're gettin' at. I mean, I'm not invited. I'm workin'. I
mean, I'm not a guest or anythin'.

BETTY: Yeah, I know all that. I'm not sayin' anythin'.

EDDIE: Well, you're lookin' at me as if to say somethin'!

BETTY: What?

EDDIE: Ah, look, nothin'. Forget it. I'd be better be gettin'
back.

He rises to put on his jacket.

BETTY: You're as touchy lately. It's like walkin' on eggshells
talkin' to yeh. I mean, what's supposed to be wrong
with yeh anyway?

EDDIE: I don't know. I've just sort of a feelin' about this
one, yeh know.

BETTY: But sure, why don't yeh just get out of it?

EDDIE: I don't think I can anymore. It's as if the story's
already begun. Yeh know? And I'm sort of locked into it
or somethin'.

BETTY: But sure, that's ridiculous, Eddie.

EDDIE: Yeah, I know it is, but that's the way I feel. Listen,
I'm goin' to go. I'll see yeh tonight some time, yeah?
He kisses her.

BETTY: Yeah. Be careful, won't yeh.

EDDIE: I'll be all right . . . See yeh.

EDDIE *leaves.* BETTY's *face as the noise of the wedding in the background becomes more prominent.*

EXT. ORCHARD. DAY.
The wedding. A red-haired, freckled faced TRAVELLER *is singing, the little showband accompanying her.*

TRAVELLER (*sings*): They say love is like a flower/ Even when it's new/ But love is like a flower/ Only when it's true/ And then love is like a diamond/ But they haven't got a clue/ Love can take you to the stars/ Then love makes a fool of you

Once I had a lover/ Who swore his love was true/ He left me for another/ Made his baby blue/ Now my heart is full of thunder/ But what am I to do?/ You'll know what I'm talking about/ When love makes a fool of you. *We travel from face to face –* JOHN, KATHLEEN, GINGER, DERMOT, SHIRLEY, CAROL, EDDIE, GERRY *and his wife* ROSY, LADY CASH *and the other freckled faced travellers. The poignancy of the lyrics do not go unnoticed. During the song* DERMOT *asks* KATHLEEN *up to dance. She looks to* JOHN *who half-heartedly approves. Before departing hand in hand with* DERMOT *she finds herself staring into the wise old eyes of* LADY CASH. KATHLEEN *quickly averts her gaze for fear the old woman can read her mind. The young couple dance.*

JOHN: What do yeh think of her, Lady?

LADY CASH: I don't know, John. To tell yeh the truth, I was sort of hopin' you'd fall for a slightly older woman this time round.

JOHN (*chuckles*): Next time, Lady. (*Sad pause.*) But sure, maybe it'll all work out all right with the help of the Lord.

LADY CASH: Aye maybe. At the same time, John.

45

LADY CASH *moves away.* JOHN *watches her go. Then he*
turns to watch the young dancing couple out on the floor.
SONG: Her face in every flower/ Her name on every rose/
You need her arms around you/ When the cold wind
blows/ You think that you're in heaven/ But you haven't
got a clue/ Love can take you to the stars/ Then love
makes a fool of you.
Laughter. JOHN *looks around, afraid that they are*
laughing at him.

EXT. ORCHARD. DANCE FLOOR. DAY.
DERMOT *and* KATHLEEN *are dancing.* EDDIE *watches them,*
fearful for the future. The young couple are gazing earnestly
into each other's eyes, talking all the time. EDDIE *looks across*
at JOHN *who seems to turn away, full of pain.* EDDIE *looks*
back at the young couple again. He tries to read their lips. And
then something happens – DERMOT *lets her go and walks away*
from her so that she is left alone, in the middle of the dance
floor, feeling a little foolish. The song has ended and the band
play another slow waltz. The dance floor is suddenly swamped
with people.

KATHLEEN (*calling out over the noise*): Dermot . . .
Dermot . . .
EDDIE*'s face as he watches her, one eye on* DERMOT *as he*
leaves the wedding.

EXT. ORCHARD. NIGHT.
The wedding. Night has fallen and only a few drunken
stragglers remain. JOHN *is talking to another* TRAVELLER
with GERRY *close by.* LADY CASH *and* ROSY *are conversing*
in the background.

JOHN: He was as tough as nails.

GERRY: Strongest man I ever met.

TRAVELLER: I heard that all right.

JOHN (*to* TRAVELLER): I mean, Gerry here is strong, but he couldn't hold a candle to my Dada. (*To* GERRY.) I mean, yeh couldn't hold a candle to my Dada, right?

GERRY (*shaking his head*): I could not.

JOHN (*chuckles*): The old bastard. Where is he now?

TRAVELLER: Well, Gerry, are yeh all set for Saturday?

GERRY: Yeah. Set as I'll ever be.

TRAVELLER: Fair play to yeh, boy.

EDDIE *pushes down the lid on the suitcase of money, cramming in the overflowing notes. He takes the suitcase to* JOHN.

JOHN: The lad better be 'cause I'm going to slap every penny of this on him. And I want to see teeth and hair flyin' in all directions.

The men laugh. KATHLEEN *stands nearby.*

KATHLEEN: I'm goin' into the house.

JOHN: Right. Right, Kathleen. I'll, I'll, um . . . I'll be there in a minute.

They watch her go. An awkward silence. And then a few titters.

JOHN: What? (*To* TRAVELLER.) . . . Isn't it well for me, boy?

Laughter.

TRAVELLER: Fair play to yeh, John . . .

KATHLEEN *disappears into the shadow of the house.*
JOHN *closes the case, hands it to* EDDIE *and gives him the bend to go with her.*

EXT. FRONT OF HOUSE. NIGHT.

EDDIE *and* KATHLEEN *are going towards the front door of the house.* EDDIE *is carrying the case of money.* KATHLEEN *seems a bit down in herself.* EDDIE *wonders about her.*

EDDIE: Are yeh all right?

KATHLEEN: Why wouldn't I be?

EDDIE (*tapping the case of money*): No reason.

> *She turns, looks at him and snatches the suitcase from his arms.*

KATHLEEN: I think you'd better go back to the party, boy.

> EDDIE *sees* DERMOT *in the house. He looks somewhat sinister.* KATHLEEN *looks at* EDDIE *to signify that she wants him to go.* EDDIE *sighs and reluctantly leaves, glancing back over his shoulder as he goes, sensing trouble in store for himself. And then* KATHLEEN *and* DERMOT *are alone.*

EXT. STREET. NIGHT.

EDDIE, *driving the Mercedes, pulls in outside of* LADY CASH's *house, a huge place with garish arches and Dallas-style design. Her married son stuffs a five pound note into* EDDIE's *top pocket.* EDDIE *secretly resents it.*

EDDIE: Cheers.

MARRIED SON: You're welcome.

> EDDIE *sits in the car until they have all gone inside. He opens up the glove compartment and takes out a bar of Aero. He eats it, throws the wrapper out of the window.*

EXT. SCRAPYARD. NIGHT.

EDDIE *pulls into the scrapyard in the Mercedes. He gets out.* GINGER *is standing in the doorway of the little house.* REG, *in his Sunday suit, is standing on the elevated landing while a few stragglers from* GERRY's *family hang around the yard.* EDDIE *senses that there is trouble in the air.*

GINGER: What do you want?

EDDIE (*to* GINGER): I just brought back the car.

48

GINGER: Take the keys up to him.

He indicates the office. EDDIE *slowly goes up the stairs nodding to* REG *as he passes.*

INT. OFFICE. NIGHT.

EDDIE *enters the office. Another few stragglers from* GERRY's *family hang around. It feels like a funeral. There is no sign of* GERRY *and* JOHN. *We can hear their voices coming from behind the curtain.* EDDIE *goes to it and peers in through the opening.*

GERRY: Jaysus, I'm terrible sorry about this John.
Disgraced the family, she did. And as for that other fella
. . . he's dead.

JOHN *sees* EDDIE *and comes to him.*

JOHN: Where have yeh been?

EDDIE: I had to drive Mrs Cash home.

JOHN: What did yeh tell me yeh did with the money again?

EDDIE: Gave it to Kathleen.

JOHN: What about Dermot?

EDDIE: Dermot? I never saw Dermot.

JOHN *looks deep into his eyes.*

JOHN: Wait outside with the rest of them.

EDDIE *gives him the keys and exits.* JOHN *is speaking in Shelta.*

JOHN (*in Shelta*): A townie.

TRAVELLER (*in Shelta*): A real snake in the grass, John.

EXT. SCRAPYARD. EVENING.

EDDIE *comes out onto the elevated landing to stand beside the old man. He looks down at the yard.*

EDDIE: What's goin' on?

REG: Laughin' boy is after doin' a bunk with the bride. They took the case of money and everything. Eleven grand! (*He sighs and throws his eyes to heaven.*) . . . War! Whist.

The phone is ringing inside. Someone answers it. Soon GERRY *comes out onto the landing.*

GERRY: Right, lads. The Great Southern Hotel. Let's go.

Suddenly they are all jumping into cars and vans and driving out of the yard. JOHN *comes out onto the landing.* GINGER *is alert, waiting for the order.* JOHN *watches the cars and vans driving away and then he goes sadly back inside.*

INT. BAR. NIGHT.
EDDIE *is making a phone-call, waiting for a reply.* DERMOT'S *voice comes on the other end.*

EDDIE: Hello, Dermot? It's Eddie. They know where you are Dermot. They're comin' to get yeh. (*Pause.*) I don't know. The war drums or somethin', knowin', you people. So, you'd better get out of there fairly pronto. By the way, thanks for droppin' me in it.

There was nearly eleven grand in that little suitcase, yeh know! Yeah well, yeh might be glad to know, I've been gettin' the fuckin' evil eye ever since. I mean, what the fuck were you thinkin' of? I could end up pushin' up the piss-beds here. You're goin' to have to give that money back to them, yeh know!

What do yeh mean, how come? I was responsible for that money. I mean, sooner or later they're goin' to come callin'.

And another thing, I never saw you tonight either, right? I never saw yeh! Shit, the money's goin'! I said the money's going. (*He slams down receiver.*) Bollocks!

50

INT. BEDROOM. NIGHT.

EDDIE *is lying in bed.* SHIRLEY *appears in the doorway.*

SHIRLEY (*a little tipsy*): Well, that wasn't exactly a marriage
    made in heaven, now, was it? (SHIRLEY *chuckles.*
    EDDIE *sits up suddenly.*) That makes even you and me
    look like the perfect pair. . . . Poor Eddie.

EDDIE: What's poor about me?

SHIRLEY: Yeh just keep gettin' left behind all the time. I
    mean, there's that young lad and he ended up with the
    money *and* the girl.

EDDIE: Will he live to tell the tale, though?

SHIRLEY: That's the trouble with you, Eddie, yeh want to
    live too long. I mean, yeh have to end up with the
    money and the girl, otherwise . . . (*She shrugs.*)
    Night . . .

EDDIE: Night.

She goes. EDDIE *sighs, lies back and gazes up at the
    ceiling despondently.*

INT. BEDROOM. NIGHT.

SHIRLEY *stands in the bedroom doorway, looking at the two
sleeping children. A look of tenderness and regret creeps into her
eyes. We focus in on the smallest girl as she stirs. Sensing
someone is looking in at her she opens her eyes and turns to look
towards the doorway only to find it empty.*

EXT. MOTEL. DAWN.

DERMOT *and* KATHLEEN *get out of the car in the carpark. As*
DERMOT *takes the bags from the boot (one bag, one suitcase
and the small suitcase of money)* KATHLEEN *stands around
looking on, feeling slightly awkward as she looks towards what
to her is a fancy motel.*

INT. MOTEL. ROOM. DAWN.

DERMOT *embraces* KATHLEEN. *They kiss. He lifts her up as she removes his shirt. They fall onto bed.*

EXT. WOODLANDS. DAY.

EDDIE *is standing on the hilltop overlooking the clearing. Down below we can see* JOHN POWER's *lonely figure gazing into the river.* EDDIE's *sad, understanding face.*

JOHN POWER *is standing on a big rock, gazing down at the spot where he first saw* KATHLEEN *dive. His sad, lonely face,* EDDIE *on the hilltop in the distance.*

EXT. OPEN FIELD. DAY.

A bare-knuckled fist-fight – GERRY *fighting another traveller called* MARCY. *There is blood everywhere – on their faces, on their arms, on their chests and spattered on the clothes of the noisy spectators. In the throng we see* JOHN POWER *and* GINGER, *and* EDDIE *who is busy taking bets all around him which* JOHN *seems to be discreetly monitoring.*

TRAVELLER: Yeah, yeah, yeah. Look, he bet him before, the last time, no bother.

EDDIE: Three-to-one is the odds. Take it or leave it.

GERRY (*to* MARCY): Come on!

TRAVELLER: Look, I'll tell yeh what I'll do, I'll slap five big-ones on Marcy, if yeh give me four-to-one odds.

EDDIE: I'll give yeh three-to-one odds that Gerry'll take him in three rounds or under.

TRAVELLER: Right. Okay. You're on.

The next few lines are spoken in Shelta.

SECOND TRAVELLER (*in Shelta*): Take it easy Sonny. He did it the last time.

FIRST TRAVELLER (*in Shelta*): By Jaysus, if he did it the last time then he won't do it this time.

EDDIE: Come on, come on. Show us the colour of your
money, so!

The wad of money is passed over. EDDIE *takes it, winks
across at* JOHN POWER *who nods approvingly. And then
we close in on* JOHN'S *face as he reacts to someone laughing
behind him. He looks across at the little laughing
congregation –* LADY CASH *amongst them. Her eyes meet
his – hers full of compassion, his eyes filled with pain. And
then he is smarted back to reality as* GERRY *knocks his
opponent to the ground.* MARCY *gallantly tries to rise but
does not make it.* GERRY *stands bloody and triumphant
above him.* JOHN *smiling through his pain.*

EXT. SCRAPYARD. DAY.

CAROL (*shouts to* GINGER): Well, if you're going now, don't
come back. I won't be here!

GINGER (*shouts to* CAROL): Don't be here, I tell yeh. Don't
be here. Go back to yeh old fellow then, yeh fucking rip,
yeh.

He turns and walks to van.

CAROL: They treat me better than you treat me!

CAROL *stands in doorway.* RAYMIE *loads van.* GINGER
steps towards her.

GINGER: Back in the house now, and do whatever it is
you're supposed to be doing. Dressed like that.
(GINGER *glances at* RAYMIE.) What are you fuckin'
lookin' at? (*To* CAROL.) Go in and do what you're
supposed to be doing.

GINGER *leaves in car.* RAYMIE *looks at* CAROL. *She
turns, goes into house and closes door.*

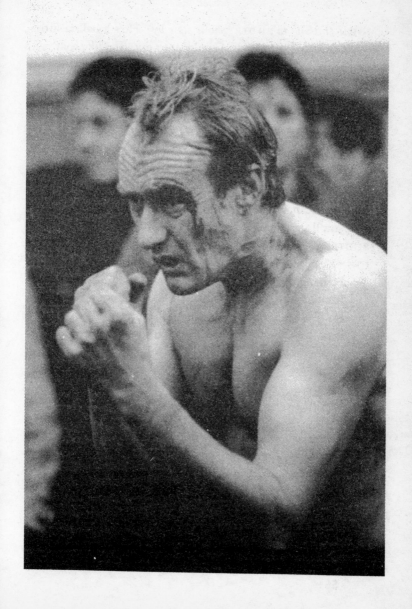

INT. OFFICE. EVENING.

JOHN *is looking out of his office window, down onto the yard below where* RAYMIE *is conversing with* REG.

JOHN (*talking to* EDDIE *who is close by*): He's a ballsie little bastard, I'll tell yeh. Comin' into my yard like that. Huh, he must be feelin' lucky or somethin'. (*Pause.*) Listen, I want to be straight with yeh. I want to see her again, hear her voice at least. And I don't care what she says to me either. Yeh know? I mean, I really don't care. Yeh know? Whatever! I'd like you to tell her that, if yeh should see her again. And yeh can tell her also that, I don't care what she's done. I'll take her back whenever she wants to come back.

I mean, I'm telling you this because, I know that, that you'll understand, like.

EDDIE: Yeah.

JOHN: Yeah. Yeah. Jesus, 'yeah' he says. Your Missus could be bangin' right in front of yeh and you'd still take her back. 'Cause you're a sucker. I mean, I know, I know, we're all suckers when it comes to women. But you take it to the extreme. You're a fuckin' double decker. I mean, you should have held on to that money, yeh know.

EDDIE: I did. I mean I just gave it to Kathleen.

JOHN: Yeh gave it to Kathleen? Not Dermot?

EDDIE: I told yeh, I never even saw Dermot.

JOHN: Just like yeh never left him alone with her that night. Just like he never walked her across the field like. I suppose you thought that was funny, you and him. Huh? And you'd better pray too, that that money is still intact when I find them. Otherwise, someone's going to get hurt around here and it ain't going to be me. Now fuck off with your 'yeah'! . . . (EDDIE *turns to door.*) And another thing, I wouldn't get too close to that other

56

fella down there, if I was you. 'Cause he don't look too lucky to me.

EDDIE's *face in the doorway, a strange look of defiance in his eyes.*

INT. WAREHOUSE. DAY.

EDDIE *is up on the stage, a crowd beneath him.* RAYMIE *is doing the running around.*

EDDIE: Aftershave for the man in your life. Perfume from Paris for behind your ear. An overnight case, just in case. We're goin' to need another bag, Raymie.

RAYMIE: Another brain'd be more like it!

EDDIE: A portable phone. So you can give him a bell whenever yeh feel like checkin' up on him. Two pairs of bedroom slippers – his and hers.

RAYMIE (*pleading*): What are yeh doin'? What are yeh doin'? What are yeh doin'?

EDDIE: I'm definitely going to need another bag, Raymie. (*Shouts.*) A tool-box for the handy man. I thought you said you were handy. I am handy, I only live around the corner.

EDDIE *spies* DERMOT *at the end of the hall.*

EXT. CARPARK. DAY.

EDDIE *and* DERMOT *approach the car where* KATHLEEN *is sitting.* RAYMIE *is packing up the van which is parked close by.* DERMOT *and* KATHLEEN *look like they have grown tired of each other.* EDDIE *nods to her. She half-heartedly nods back.*

DERMOT: I mean, I don't think I'm exactly cut-out for this eternity lark if that's what yeh mean.

EDDIE: Is the money still intact?

DERMOT: More or less. Why?

RAYMIE (*coming over, peeved*): I'm all loaded up now, Eddie. Come on, let's go and get out of here.

EDDIE: Yeah, right, I'll be there in a minute. (*He takes* DERMOT *to one side.*) Listen, she's goin' to have to go back sooner or later, yeh know that don't yeh?

DERMOT: Yeah?

EDDIE: Absolutely. And when she does you'll be left high and dry. And so will I for sidin' with yeh. Now, I got somethin' goin' on. You could take the money and come in with me – fifty-fifty down the middle. Of course you'd have to lie fairly low for a while, but at least you'll be makin' a few bob while you're down there. What do yeh think?

DERMOT (*shaking his head*): I don't know, Eddie. I mean, I don't think she wants to go back to him yet, yeh know.

EDDIE: Then you'll have to bail out.

DERMOT: Run out on her, you mean. I don't know about that. I mean, we didn't do it for the money, yeh know.

EDDIE: What did yeh do it for?

DERMOT: I don't know. Love, and all that jazz, I suppose.

EDDIE: Yeah, well, dyin' for love is one thing, Dermot – Livin' to tell the tale is another.

DERMOT: Yeah, but sure he's not goin' to let us just walk away with the money anyway.

EDDIE: We'll just tell him it's the price of love!

DERMOT (*suspicious*): I thought yeh wanted me to give it back to him?

EDDIE: Yeah, well, I changed me mind.

KATHLEEN *bamps the horn and calls out to* DERMOT.

KATHLEEN (*in Shelta*): C'mon Dermot, I'm scared.

DERMOT *makes to leave.* DERMOT *seems a little disappointed in* EDDIE*, and a little distrustful.*

DERMOT: I don't know, I'll have to think about it. We'll see.

EDDIE: Where will you be?

59

DERMOT: I don't know. I'll call yeh.

EDDIE *alone in the dust as they drive away.*

INT. WAREHOUSE. DAY.

EDDIE *is looking over a dark, dilapidated warehouse with* ARTHUR, *a forty-four-year-old Mammy's boy at his heels.*

EDDIE: How much did yeh say she's wantin' for it again?

ARTHUR: She'll be lookin' for a hundred a week for it anyway, I'd say.

EDDIE: Yeah? No, it's just that there's a few damp patches around the place, like, yeh know . . . She wouldn't drop it down to the fifty for the first year would she? Just to give me a chance to get on me feet a bit?

ARTHUR: I'd say the lowest she'd go now'd be seventy-five, like, yeh know.

EDDIE: Yeah?

ARTHUR: But sure I suppose you'd be lookin' for a place with windows and everything would yeh?

EDDIE: No, not necessarily. Windows only distract the customers, Arthur, like, yeh know.

ARTHUR: Aye?

EDDIE: Absolutely!

EDDIE: How is she keepin' anyway, Arthur?

ARTHUR: She's well, thanks. But sure I'll ask her to drop down to the fifty, if yeh like . . . Do yeh want me to?

EDDIE: Aye, I do.

ARTHUR: All right so, I'll ask her, sure. It don't cost nothin' to ask do it? Huh?

EDDIE: No.

Before they lock up, EDDIE *takes one last look, his eyes revealing his interest in the place. And then the door is banged and bolted so that we are left in the dark cavernous warehouse and for a minute we see its potential. This is where* EDDIE *will build his stage. Here is where the audience-customers will stand, etc.*

   We almost hear the babble of the crowd and the banter of 'Trojan Eddie' as he goes about his work. EDDIE*'s dream.*

EDDIE (*v.o.*): These watches are the best bargain you're ever likely to meet, 'cos I'm giving them away for nothing. One for the lady in red. One for the lady in purple. And one for the toothless wonder down at the front there.

   That's the kind of thing that happens when 'Trojan Eddie' comes to town.

INT. MOTEL. ROOM. NIGHT.
DERMOT *sits in a chair, naked. Stares at* KATHLEEN, *asleep in bed, naked.*

INT. BAR. NIGHT.
EDDIE *is sitting up at the counter in* MATT*'s place. Through the rain drenched window he sees his own sad reflection as* GINGER *and* SHIRLEY *get out of a car across the street and race hand in hand into a nearby restaurant.* EDDIE *sighs. Sad pause.*

EDDIE: Do you ever remember a fella called 'Bargain Joe', Matt?

MATT: Yeah, of course I remember 'Bargain Joe'. He used to have a stall in the market, one day a week. 'Bargain Joe', yeah! He was a nice fella.

EDDIE: I used to stand and watch that fella for hours on end when I was a little lad, yeh know. Fascinated me he did. Jaysus. (*Chuckles.*) He was a real jingler-boy. He could sell yeh somethin' yeh didn't even want, yeh know.

MATT: Yeah, I know. Flints and lighters and tin openers and all that.

61

EDDIE: I mean he wouldn't do yeh now nor nothin'. He just managed to sell yeh somethin' yeh didn't particularly need, that's all. And the banter he had. A fuckin' genius, boy! Do yeh know what his motto was? Always buy cheaper than yeh sell. Simple, yeh know. Well, I'm sort of like him now, yeh know.

MATT: Yeah?

EDDIE: Yeah. 'Trojan Eddie!' and I come out with all this spiel too. Yeh know, it just sort of spills out of me . . . Hello Mrs, fancy a canary. Goin' cheap . . . (*He laughs.*) *Pause. He ponders. A phone rings, the portable in* EDDIE's *coat pocket which is draped across the back of the chair.* RAYMIE, *returning from the toilet, answers it.*

RAYMIE: Yeah?

DERMOT: Eddie, it's Dermot. I'm out in the old caravan in Cleary's Cross in case you're lookin' for me.

RAYMIE *steps to* EDDIE.

RAYMIE: It's for you. (*He gives* EDDIE *the phone.*)

EDDIE: Hello. Dermot. Yeah? . . . What do you think? . . . Well what do you think I mean? . . . Jesus, I mean, come on! . . .

A man enters while EDDIE *is on the phone.* EDDIE *beckons to him to sit down.* RAYMIE's *suspicious, jealous face.*

INT. CARAVAN. NIGHT.

DERMOT *is sitting in the middle of a dilapidated caravan, speaking into a mobile phone. We can see* KATHLEEN *through the window outside.*

DERMOT: Yeah, I'm goin' to bail out. Pick us up tonight at the Cross, will yeh. Yeah, yeah, I'll have the money, don't worry. What do yeh think I'm goin' to do, leave it

here or somethin'? . . . Yeah, right, twelve it is. Don't
be late. . . .
*He hangs up and sighs as he gazes around at his dreary
surroundings.*

INT. BAR. NIGHT.
Back in MATT's *bar,* EDDIE *puts the mobile phone away. He
looks at* RAYMIE *and then across at the* MAN *at the table.
Pause. He goes towards the table.* RAYMIE *watching him from
afar.*

EDDIE: So what have yeh got for me?
MAN: What do you want?
EDDIE: What have you got!
  RAYMIE's *face – suspicious, jealous, angry. He leaves his
  unfinished pint on the counter, makes for the door.*
RAYMIE: See you later, Eddie.
EDDIE: Yeah, right, Raymie. Oh, listen, we may have to
  shift a bit of stuff early tomorrow morning.
RAYMIE: Yeah, right. Give us a shout sure.
  RAYMIE *leaves.* EDDIE *wonders about him.*

EXT. CLEARY'S CROSS. NIGHT.
EDDIE *is standing outside the caravan in Cleary's Cross – a
lonely crossroads in the middle of nowhere. He pushes open the
creaking door to find nobody home. He goes inside.*

INT. CARAVAN. NIGHT.
EDDIE *enters the caravan to find things in disarray. A lamp
knocked over, a bedside locker overturned, etc. A window wide
open and the curtain blowing. He looks around, peeping into the
toilet, etc. He finds the mobile phone on the floor. He picks it up
and tries it out. It is still working. He pockets it and leaves.*

63

INT. LOCK-UP. EARLY MORNING.

MAN *opens warehouse door.*

EDDIE *and* RAYMIE *are in an old lock-up, surrounded by all the usual items that he sells.* RAYMIE *opens up the back of the van and begins to load it up.* EDDIE, *a little dubious, is standing by the window, surveying the room.*

MAN (*to* EDDIE): Now, take whatever yeh want and, er, I'll see yeh later. Oh, and leave the old telly, won't yeh?

    MAN *turns, walks off.*

EDDIE (*to* MAN): Will yeh be coming back?

MAN (*shouts*): Yeah, I'll be back in about ten minutes.

EDDIE: I don't know whether to take all this stuff now, or not.

RAYMIE: That's what we came here for, ain't it?

EDDIE: That's the trouble with you, Raymie, you never lose any sleep.

RAYMIE (*going about his work*): I'm not goin' to lose any sleep over that little prick anyway, that's for sure. Why, do yeh think he's goin' to lose any sleep over you?

EDDIE (*he looks out of the window*): . . . Where is he though? That's what I'd like to know.

RAYMIE: Ah, fuck him!

INT. EDDIE'S HOUSE. EARLY MORNING.

EDDIE *enters his own living room. He goes to the window to draw back the curtains and is startled to find* DERMOT *stretched out on the couch.* DERMOT *sits up, moaning and wincing with pain.* EDDIE'S *eyes light up at the sight of him.*

EDDIE: Dermot. . . ! What happened?

DERMOT: The McDonaghs came after us.

EDDIE: The McDonaghs?

64

DERMOT: Yeah. As if I wasn't bad enough with her people and the Powers lookin' for me, now the McDonaghs want to get in on the act. I think I cracked a rib tryin' to get away from them.

EDDIE: Where's Kathleen?

DERMOT: She's upstairs, havin' a wash.

EDDIE *sighs with relief.*

EDDIE: So, where's the money?

DERMOT: The money's gone, Eddie.

EDDIE: What do yeh mean, it's gone?

DERMOT: We had to leave it behind us sure. The McDonaghs probably have it by now.

EDDIE: You're joking me right? (DERMOT *shakes his head.*) You're joking me! Shit! . . . I don't believe it, yeh fuckin' eejit yeh!

DERMOT: Sure, what could I do? I mean, they were stormin' in on top of us.

EDDIE: I don't believe it . . . I do not believe it. I'm after getting a rake of stuff on the strength of . . . (*Shouts.*) Of course, yeh know what I should've done, I should've . . . Oh, fuck!

DERMOT: How did they know where to find us is what I'd like to know.

Suddenly it dawns on EDDIE. *A quick flash of the McDonaghs piling into the caravan, past the camera.*

DERMOT: What?

A rustle at the front door. EDDIE *is startled.*

EDDIE: Shirley!

SHIRLEY *enters, stands in the doorway.* DERMOT *smiles at her.*

SHIRLEY: Well, what do yeh know, the fugitive of love, huh!

EDDIE *throws her a disgusted look.* SHIRLEY *resents it.*

SHIRLEY: What's wrong with you?

EDDIE: Ah, go to bed, will yeh?

SHIRLEY: Do you know, I think I will. After all, when a
man leaves a woman with her legs in the air to go
running back to his little misses it's time to call it a day I
think, don't you?

KATHLEEN *is coming down the stairs and into the living
room to sit close to* DERMOT. SHIRLEY *looks up at her
with contempt. Then she turns to* EDDIE *with a vengeance.*

SHIRLEY: You're even a bigger eejit than I thought yeh
were . . . Mind you, one thing I will say for Dermot
though, is that least he'd never leave a woman with her
legs in the air. Would yeh, Dermot?

EDDIE *is offended as he looks into her dark, angry eyes.*

EDDIE: What are you on about?

SHIRLEY: Jesus, you're slow.

DERMOT: Don't mind her, Eddie.

EDDIE *throws him a dagger of a look.* SHIRLEY *leaves
the room.* EDDIE *follows her.*

INT. HALL AND STAIRS. EARLY MORNING.
SHIRLEY *is going up the stairs.* EDDIE *is standing at the
bottom of the stairs.*

EDDIE: You bitch.
You come back here to traipse in and out like yeh
owned the place or somethin' – makin' a fool of me,
(*shouts*) hardly lookin' at the children.

SHIRLEY: So what if I'm an unfit mother, sue me. You're no
great shakes yourself.

EDDIE (*following her up the stairs*): I do me best at least.

SHIRLEY: Tell it to the judge.

EDDIE: What did you say?

SHIRLEY (*stopping to face him, defiantly*): You heard me.

EDDIE: You try and come between me and those children
and I swear to God . . .

SHIRLEY: All right, Eddie keep your shirt on. I'm not even sure they're both yours, for Christ's sake.

EDDIE pounces on her, punching her in the mouth. He hits her again and as she crawls along the landing on all fours to try and get away from him he is slapping her and kicking her etc.

EDDIE: You bitch . . . you good for nothin'. . . .

DERMOT (*at the foot of the stairs*): Take it easy Eddie. Eddie!

EDDIE: Look just get out of here will yeh!

DERMOT: Jesus, Eddie.

EDDIE (*shouts*): GET THE FUCK OUT OF HERE!

KATHLEEN: Come on Dermot . . . let's go . . . Let's get out of here . . .

She gathers the coats etc and then she stands to look disdainfully up into EDDIE's face.

DERMOT (*looking pleadingly up into EDDIE's sad eyes*): Jaysus, Eddie, yeh know me!

DERMOT and KATHLEEN leave. SHIRLEY is crouched on the floor of the little box-room wiping the blood from her mouth. EDDIE looks into the other room to see the girls in their night clothes, huddled together, terrified. EDDIE's eyes brim with tears.

JENNY: Are you all right, Daddy?

EDDIE: Yeah, it's all right lads . . . Everything's all right . . .

INT. BEDROOM. EARLY MORNING.
BETTY's *face. Through the window we can see* SHIRLEY *coming out of* EDDIE's *house across the road and struggling down the street with her bags and suitcase.* BETTY's *face by the window.*

EXT. HALTING SITE. DAY.

PATSY MCDONAGH *comes running out the back door of a caravan. He runs in to* GINGER *who knocks him to the ground with the butt of a shotgun.* JOHN POWER *appears in the doorway behind him.*

GINGER: Where's our money?

PATSY: What money? I didn't see any money. I swear.

GINGER (*pointing the gun at him*): Where's our fucking money?

PATSY: I don't know what you're talking about!

JOHN (*going to him*): I thought I told you to get out of here.

PATSY: Yeah, I know, but I don't know no-one over there.

GERRY *appears in the doorway behind.*

GERRY: There's nothing here, John.

Pause. JOHN *takes the shotgun from* GINGER *and goes over and shoots one of the horses in the head. It falls with a limp thud. The little crowd that has gathered gasp.*

JOHN (*tossing the gun back to* GINGER): Where did yeh say the money was?

PATSY: Maybe the townie has it. Trojan Eddie. Kathleen said that Dermot was on the phone to him a couple of times.

Pause. JOHN *looks around from face to face and makes to leave.* TRAVELLING WOMAN *follows him, smiles, singing.*

TRAVELLING WOMAN (*calling after them*): Maids, when you're young never wed an old man/ 'Cos he's got no valourum/ He's lost his dingdorum/ Maids, when you're young, never wed an old man/ He's got no valourum/ He's lost his dingdorum/ Maids, when you're young never wed an old man.

JOHN POWER'S *wounded face as he walks away from the throng and drives off.*

69

INT. BACK YARD. EARLY MORNING.

RAYMIE *stacking boxes at the rear of* EDDIE's *new warehouse.*

RAYMIE: So, yeh think I snitched on him, is that it?

EDDIE: Did yeh?

RAYMIE: What are yeh sidin' with him all the time for? He's no friend of yours. You could be on fire and he wouldn't even cross the road to piss on yeh.

EDDIE: What did they give yeh, Raymie? Twenty quid, thirty, forty, what?

RAYMIE: Let it rest will yeh. I mean you didn't hear me complainin' when he was brought in instead of me. I let it rest.

EDDIE (*growing really dark*): There was nearly eleven grand in that little suitcase. Can you understand that?

RAYMIE: Yeah I think I can understand that all right, Eddie.

EDDIE (*grabbing him*): Well, understand this, (*shouts*) thanks to you I'm back on the street again.

RAYMIE (*breaking his grip, furious*): So what, Eddie? Do you want me to lose some sleep over it or somethin'? Just like you lost sleep when you were tryin' to freeze me out. (*Shouts.*) Freezin' me out! Your best fucking friend! For a tinker!

EDDIE (*shouts*): I did time for you.

RAYMIE: No, Eddie, you got caught. You always got caught. I'm to blame 'cause you got caught! Well, now you're caught again, Eddie. You've a roomful of stuff and no money to pay for it. So what are yeh goin' to do? Give it all back. (*Chuckles.*) Tell the man you're sorry? I mean, I know I done some queer things on yeh in me time and all, Eddie, but there was things I didn't do on yeh too, yeh know.

EDDIE: What do yeh mean?

RAYMIE: Let it rest, will yeh.

Pause. EDDIE *goes to the toilet.* RAYMIE *watches him go, affection and sadness in his eyes.*

INT. TOILET. EARLY MORNING.
EDDIE *is washing his hands. Footsteps outside and then voices.*

RAYMIE: How's it goin'?
GINGER: How's it goin'?
> EDDIE *instinctively pastes himself to the wall behind the toilet door. He looks out through the crack in the open door.*

INT. WAREHOUSE. EARLY MORNING.

GINGER: Where's the other fella?
RAYMIE: He's out.
GINGER (*looking around*): What's goin' on?
RAYMIE: Opposition, Ginger. Tell your Da his days are numbered.
GINGER: He must have come into a bit of money or somethin', did he?
RAYMIE: Yeah, a bit of a windfall, Ginger, like, yeh know. A bit of a windfall, boy!
GINGER: You're a smirky little bastard. Anyone ever tell yeh that?
RAYMIE: Yeah, I have a dirty kind of a smile all right, haven't I? But sure, what harm?
GINGER (*turning away*): Little prick.
RAYMIE: Now, who told you that?
GINGER: What?
RAYMIE: Naw, I'm only kiddin' yeh.
> GINGER *turns dark and dangerous. He watches* RAYMIE *from behind. Suddenly he picks up a sharp hook and rams*

72

it into the side of RAYMIE's *neck.* RAYMIE *gasps and stumbles to the floor.*

GINGER: I want to talk to you. (*Pushes* RAYMIE's *face against the mirror.*) That sort of wiped the smirk off your face, didn't it? Huh? (*Shouts.*) Didn't it? I don't see yeh smilin' now, yeh fuckin' little prick yeh – laughin' at me! You, laughing at me! I don't think so!

RAYMIE *slides down the blood-stained mirror and lays himself gently down, bleeding all over the ground, crawling to try and get away from* GINGER's *shuffling feet, dragging his body through the muddy puddles of rain.* GINGER *follows him about the yard, smirking at his handiwork until he realises that things are serious.*

He backs away, looking down to discover that RAYMIE *has bled all over his shoes, turning to see his own bloody footprints all over the place. He tries desperately to erase them with his feet but he only makes matters worse. And then* ARTHUR *appears.* GINGER *sees him.* ARTHUR *flees.* GINGER *panics and runs for it, his bloody footprints all over the place.*

INT. TOILET. MORNING.
We see GINGER *leaving from* EDDIE's *perspective behind the door.*

EXT. BACK YARD. MORNING.
EDDIE *comes out to cradle the dying* RAYMIE *in his arms as* RAYMIE *calls his name.*

EXT. COUNTRY ROAD. DAY.
DERMOT *is hitching along a country road. A farmer and his wife stop to pick him up. He gets into the back and they drive away.*

EXT. WILD REEDS. EVENING.

GINGER *is being led out of the wild reeds, handcuffed to a few hefty policemen. He looks bedraggled, and just as glad to be caught.* PATSY MCDONAGH *stands on the bank, looking on.*

GINGER (*to* POLICEMAN): Oh, don't beat me, sir. Don't beat me.

EXT. GRAVEYARD. DAY.

RAYMIE's *funeral.* EDDIE *and* MOTHER *and* BETTY *are coming down the aisle of the cemetery.*

Behind them we can see a little gathering collected around the grave. EDDIE *sees* JOHN POWER *beneath a tree across the way and goes to him.*

EXT. GRAVEYARD. DAY.

JOHN POWER *beneath the tree.* EDDIE *coming to him.*

JOHN: Are yeh after goin' into mourning or what?

EDDIE: How do yeh mean?

JOHN: Well, I haven't seen yeh around, like, for a few days. (EDDIE *sighs and turns away.*) Look, if this is about the other little shit bag, I wouldn't worry about it if I were you. He was trying to pull the wool over all our eyes. Did you know he was with the McDonaghs the night they went after Dermot. And for what? Thirty pieces of silver that he probably never even got.

A quick flash of the McDonaghs ransacking the caravan, the curtain fluttering. RAYMIE *is amongst them. And then* EDDIE's *disappointed face again.*

JOHN: What is it with you anyway? I mean, I took you in off the street when no one else'd even look at yeh. A feckin' little jailbird be Jaysus!

EDDIE: I made money for you, mate. Like, a lot of money.

75

JOHN: You cost me a lot of money too, I don't mind tellin'
yeh. Like, eleven grand. Does that ring a bell? Eleven
grand!

EDDIE: I don't know anythin' about that.

JOHN: That's not what I heard. And in the meantime you're
drivin' around in my van. (*Chuckles.*) Jaysus, I must be
goin' soft in the head or somethin'.

EDDIE: Yeh want the van back? Here, take it. Stick it.
(EDDIE *thrusts the keys at him.*)

JOHN (*chuckles*): Jesus, you know, we used to laugh at you.
You made our lives worth livin'!

EDDIE: What, and you think no-one's laughin' at you or
somethin'?

JOHN: What did yeh say? Mm? What did yeh say? (*He grabs
him by the collar.*) I tell yeh, if I find out you're mixed
up in all of this, I swear to Jaysus, I'll swing for you.
EDDIE *breaks free. He stands and looks into* JOHN's *eyes
and there is a certain compassion in* EDDIE's *face as he
walks away.*

JOHN: Come back you little toerag, I'm not finished with
you yet. You've no right, turning your back and walking
away from me like that. (*Shouts.*) 'Cos you don't stand a
chance without me. You haven't got a hope in hell! You
see, I know who I am, and what I am, and what I'm
worth. But you, you haven't a clue, not an idea. None
whatsoever . . . You'll come crawling back on your
belly, boy . . . You just wait and see . . . 'Trojan Eddie'
– trojan fucking eejit!
EDDIE's *face as he walks away.* JOHN POWER *in the
background jerking and twisting and pointing, his whole
body going into abuse.*

EXT. MARKET. DAY.

We are in a busy market. Fruit stalls and knick-knack stalls, fish stalls and book stalls, etc. Canopies and umbrellas overhead and hand painted signs. Tattoos and goldfish and canaries going cheap!

This is a magical scene with the camera zigzagging in and around the stalls, past tea-drinking traders and complaining customers and young girls trying on flimsy dresses over their own clothes, and a tape stall playing corny country music.

EDDIE *is working a little stall, a crowd around him. He has a little 'Kiss Me Quick' hat on his head and a huge umbrella overhead with 'Trojan Eddie' emblazoned on it.*

EDDIE: Pencils. Fifty pence a dozen. I mean, you know what they say, 'You can ride a horse to water but a pencil must be lead!' Fifty pence and I'll throw in an old rubber. Yes! One, two, three. Away yeh go, lads, before they change their minds. Now, candles. A box of twenty for a pound. I have it on good authority that there's goin' to be plenty of cuts this winter, so don't be stuck. And if you're one that lights the odd candle in the chapel every day then think of the money you'll save. One, two, three, four, five. Lock the doors, they're comin' in the windows.

BETTY *looking out at him from under the canvas of the stall. Daughters sitting with him.*

DAUGHTER (*to* EDDIE): I thought yeh said these anoraks were waterproof, Daddy.

EDDIE: I never said they were waterproof. Waterproof, for a pound, give me a break!

BETTY *smiles.*

INT. WAREHOUSE. DAY.

EDDIE *is down at the far end of the room packing all the stuff back into boxes etc.* ARTHUR *enters.*

ARTHUR: There's someone here to see yeh, boss.

EDDIE: What's that? (*He stands as he sees* KATHLEEN.) Oh yeah, right. Thanks.

ARTHUR: You'll pull over that old door after yeh, won't yeh?

EDDIE: Yeah . . . Thanks, Arthur.

ARTHUR *leaves.* KATHLEEN *comes a little deeper into the warehouse.* EDDIE *goes to his coat and takes out a flask of tea. He pours her out a cup and beckons her to come closer. She does, takes the tea and drinks.*

EDDIE: Where's Dermot?

KATHLEEN: He's after bailing out on me. Bad luck may he never shun.

EXT. SCRAPYARD. DAY.

EDDIE *and* KATHLEEN *are standing in the middle of the scrapyard.* REG, *the old man stops work to look at them. So does* CAROL *who is busy polishing the knocker.* EDDIE *gives* KATHLEEN *the bend to go up the wooden stairs. She does.* EDDIE *watches her go. Then he looks up at the office window where he can see* JOHN POWER *sitting at his desk.* JOHN's *head comes up from his work as the office door opens. Pause.*

JOHN *looks out of the window, down at* EDDIE. *Pause.*

EDDIE *looks at* CAROL *and leaves.*

INT. DILAPIDATED BUILDING. HALL. DAY.

MRS CROSBIE (RAYMIE's *old landlady*) *goes down the hall to open the front door.* EDDIE *is on the other side.*

MRS CROSBIE: Hi, Eddie. Come in.

EDDIE *enters and follows* MRS CROSBIE *up the stairs to* RAYMIE's *room.*

MRS CROSBIE: Like, it's just that my husband has someone comin' to look at the place tomorrow night, yeh know, so . . . I thought you might like to have his few bits and pieces.

EDDIE: Thanks.

MRS CROSBIE: Right, well shall I leave yeh to it, so? . . . Sure, poor Raymie wasn't the worst of them at all, yeh know. Give us a shout on your way out.

She goes. EDDIE *looks around the room at* RAYMIE's *odds and ends. He goes to the window and looks down at the dingy back street below, the sound of the street drifting up. He sits down on the side of the bed and ponders, picking up a letter, reading it. The camera travels around the room showing us the useless collection of* RAYMIE's *wasted life. Then on top of the wardrobe we spy a little familiar suitcase. On closer inspection we realise that it is* EDDIE's *old suitcase.*

Back to EDDIE, *who is suddenly blessed with an almost divine inspiration; a quick flashback to the caravan,* RAYMIE *reaching under the bed for the case of money and then back to* EDDIE's *radiant face as he looks towards the wardrobe.*

INT. CINEMA. NIGHT.

KATHLEEN *is at the counter buying an ice cream and Coke, etc. She is heavily pregnant. She walks towards the foyer to* JOHN *who is waiting for her, he helps her with the sweets and they enter the cinema. As they walk off a crowd of young people begin to laugh.* JOHN *looks over his shoulder, afraid they are laughing at him.*

INT. CINEMA. NIGHT.

JOHN *and* KATHLEEN *are sitting in the cinema. The ads are running. Suddenly we see* EDDIE's *face on the screen as he walks through a warehouse of stuff.*

EDDIE (*on screen*): What you want, I got. And if you can get it cheaper anywhere else then I want to know about it. 'Trojan Eddie's the name, bargain-zinies the game! A Walkman? I got it! A razor? I got it! A guitar? I got it! A flask? I got it! A keyboard? Had one last week. Too late. So listen, don't be done out of it, get down here now! 'Trojan Eddie's of William Street. Now!

Another short ad follows and then suddenly EDDIE's *face appears up on the screen again. A real close-up shot of him.*

EDDIE: What are yeh doin' sitting there? I said now!

JOHN's *face in the half light.*

Methuen Modern Plays

include work by

Jean Anouilh
John Arden
Margaretta D'Arcy
Peter Barnes
Sebastian Barry
Brendan Behan
Edward Bond
Bertolt Brecht
Howard Brenton
Simon Burke
Jim Cartwright
Caryl Churchill
Noël Coward
Sarah Daniels
Nick Dear
Shelagh Delaney
David Edgar
Dario Fo
Michael Frayn
John Godber
Paul Godfrey
David Greig
John Guare
Peter Handke
Jonathan Harvey
Iain Heggie
Declan Hughes
Terry Johnson
Sarah Kane
Charlotte Keatley
Barrie Keeffe
Robert Lepage
Stephen Lowe

Doug Lucie
Martin McDonagh
John McGrath
David Mamet
Patrick Marber
Arthur Miller
Mtwa, Ngema & Simon
Tom Murphy
Phyllis Nagy
Peter Nichols
Joseph O'Connor
Joe Orton
Louise Page
Joe Penhall
Luigi Pirandello
Stephen Poliakoff
Franca Rame
Mark Ravenhill
Philip Ridley
Reginald Rose
David Rudkin
Willy Russell
Jean-Paul Sartre
Sam Shepard
Wole Soyinka
C. P. Taylor
Theatre de Complicite
Theatre Workshop
Sue Townsend
Judy Upton
Timberlake Wertenbaker
Victoria Wood

Methuen World Classics

Aeschylus (two volumes)
Jean Anouilh
John Arden (two volumes)
Arden & D'Arcy
Aristophanes (two volumes)
Aristophanes & Menander
Brendan Behan
Aphra Behn
Edward Bond (five volumes)
Bertolt Brecht
  (five volumes)
Büchner
Bulgakov
Calderón
Anton Chekhov
Noël Coward (five volumes)
Eduardo De Filippo
David Edgar (three volumes)
Euripides (three volumes)
Dario Fo (two volumes)
Michael Frayn (two volumes)
Max Frisch
Gorky
Harley Granville Barker
  (two volumes)
Henrik Ibsen (six volumes)
Terry Johnson
Lorca (three volumes)
Marivaux

Mustapha Matura
David Mercer (two volumes)
Arthur Miller
  (five volumes)
Anthony Minghella
  (two volumes)
Molière
Tom Murphy
  (three volumes)
Musset
Peter Nichols (two volumes)
Clifford Odets
Joe Orton
Louise Page
A. W. Pinero
Luigi Pirandello
Stephen Poliakoff
  (two volumes)
Terence Rattigan
Ntozake Shange
Sophocles (two volumes)
Wole Soyinka
David Storey (two volumes)
August Strindberg
  (three volumes)
J. M. Synge
Ramón del Valle-Inclán
Frank Wedekind
Oscar Wilde